WS

The Henry A. Wallace Series
on Agricultural History and Rural Life

IOWA STATE UNIVERSITY PRESS / AMES

The Henry A. Wallace Series
on Agricultural History and Rural Life

R. Douglas Hurt, SERIES EDITOR

The Agricultural Transition
in New York State

The Agricultural Transition in New York State

MARKETS AND MIGRATION IN
MID-NINETEENTH-CENTURY AMERICA

Donald H. Parkerson

The Henry A. Wallace Series
on Agricultural History and Rural Life

IOWA STATE UNIVERSITY PRESS / AMES

DONALD H. PARKERSON is assistant professor of history
at East Carolina University, Greenville, North Carolina.

© 1995 Iowa State University Press, Ames, Iowa 50014
All rights reserved

∞ Printed on acid-free paper in the United States of America

First edition, 1995

Library of Congress Cataloging-in-Publication Data

Parkerson, Donald Hugh
    The agricultural transition in New York State: markets and migration in mid-nineteenth-century America/Donald H. Parkerson—1st ed.
        p.   cm.   —(The Henry A. Wallace series on agricultural history and rural life)
    Includes bibliographical references (p.   ).
    ISBN 0-8138-2492-3
    1. Agriculture—Economic aspects—New York (State)—History—19th century. 2. Farmers—New York (State)—History—19th century. 3. Rural-urban migration—New York (State)—History—19th century. 4. New York (State)—Economic conditions. 5. New York (State)—Social conditions. 6. New York (State)—History. 7. United States—Economic conditions. 8. United States—Social conditions. I. Title. II. Series.
HD1775.N8P37   1995
338.1'09747'09034—dc20   95-16272

To Jo

Contents

Series Editor's Introduction

Agricultural markets have been important to American farmers since the seventeenth century, especially in the South. Access to markets enabled surplus production for the sake of profit rather than subsistence, and farmers took advantage of these opportunities whenever possible. Until now, however, no historian has analyzed the origin and development of commercial agriculture in the state of New York.

In this study Donald H. Parkerson skillfully traces the emergence of commercial agriculture in New York during the mid-nineteenth century. After the Panic of 1837, farmers realized that the value of land lay not in its resale price but in the value of the crops that could be produced on it. In addition, both international and domestic affairs encouraged New York farmers to produce a surplus and specialize in order to take advantage of high prices. Between 1840 and 1865, for example, agricultural prices increased at nearly twice the rate of the prices of manufactured goods. This was due, in part, to increased immigration,—particularly from Ireland—as well as markets created by the Crimean and Civil wars. As prices rose, farmers experienced a "golden age."

With money in their pockets, farm families joined the new age of consumerism and bought plows, mowing machines, seeders, furniture, carpets, and wallpaper, as well as other agricultural equipment and household goods. Not every farm family, of course, instantly converted from practicing safety-first agriculture, that is, subsistence or self-sufficiency (so far as was possible), to commercial agriculture. Nevertheless, many began to do so on a scale and with a speed that best met their family needs. No matter the degree of participation in the market economy, by 1865 more than two-thirds of the farmers in New York embraced commercial agriculture and the economic and social changes that came with it. As these farmers increasingly produced a surplus for sale, they began to apply scientific and business practices to their agricultural operations. They also began to specialize, shifting away from grain crops to dairying and wool production.

Parkerson does more than trace the development of the market economy in New York. He also explores the relationship between migration and social change. He finds that commercially oriented farmers in New York were highly mobile as well as firmly committed to maintaining traditional family values and social relationships, such as using both kith and kin to help with the harvest in order to increase production. Above all, Parkerson is interested in individual initiative and action as he analyzes family relationships, residency, landownership, and tenancy in relation to migration and commercial agriculture. He concludes, in part, that during the mid-nineteenth century the people in rural New York were in constant motion as they moved toward opportunity in the countryside as well as in the towns and cities. For farm families, successful migration depended on timing and destination as well as extended family support. When farm families moved, however, they usually sought opportunities to tailor farm production to the needs of the market economy.

Parkerson has based his study on the analysis of the New York censuses of 1855 and 1865 and manuscript sources that enable the evaluation of individual actions as well as broad social and economic changes among New York farm families as they committed to the market economy. In doing so, he has made an important, original contribution to our understanding of American agricultural and rural history during the nineteenth century.

—R. DOUGLAS HURT

Acknowledgments

Over the last several years I have received a great deal of financial support, encouragement, and constructive criticism.

I received generous funding from the American Historical Association, Albert Beveridge Grant; the Newberry Library, Exxon Fellowship; The Economic History Association, Arthur Cole Grant; East Carolina University, Research and Travel Grants; and the Department of History, Brewster Scholar Fellowship.

Parts of this work have been presented at meetings of the Social Science History Association; the History Roundtable at East Carolina University; American Historical Association, Pacific Coast; and the Economic History Workshop at the University of Chicago.

I would like to thank Richard Jensen, Daniel Scott Smith, Robert Fogel, David Galenson, Allan Kulikoff, Peter Knights, John Adams, Alice Kasakoff, Richard Steckel, Michael Haines, Myron Gutmann, Gerard Bouchard, Randy Widdis, David Davenport, Alice Goldstein, Sidney Goldstein, Farley Grubb, Robert Swierenga, and the anonymous reviewers from Iowa State University Press for their comments and encouragement.

I would also like to thank my colleagues at East Carolina University—Kenneth Wilburn, Carl Swanson, Charles Calhoun, Todd Savitt, and Michael Palmer—for their important insights, comments, and support. Special thanks are due to Ken Wilburn, for his photography, and Brad Rogers, who drew the map for Appendix 1.

I also wish to thank Jessica Young, Anna Matthews, Cliff Morgan, and Kristen Lanier, who provided research assistance at various stages of this project. The librarians at Joyner Library at East Carolina University and Davis Memorial Library at Methodist College also have been very helpful. Special thanks to Pat Guyette, Joyner Library, interlibrary loan. I also thank the computer staff at East Carolina University, especially Barney Jernigan, Marsha Shepherd, and Ernie Marshburn.

And finally, I express my deepest appreciation to Jo Ann Parkerson for her support and invaluable assistance. This book could not have been written without her.

The Agricultural Transition
in New York State

*New farm implements, such as McCormick's reaper, helped some
nineteenth-century farmers make the transition
to surplus market farming.*

CHAPTER 1

Farmers in Transition

One of the defining characteristics of mid-nineteenth-century New York State was the extraordinary mobility of its rural people. Indeed, the frenetic pace of modern life was born and nurtured in the countryside and, to borrow a phrase, moved to the city.[1] Mid-nineteenth-century New York farmers crossed and recrossed the rural landscape and in so doing helped change fundamentally the social and economic life of their state and nation.

Born in the first decades of the nineteenth century, the men and women of this generation embraced the market economy, tasted the forbidden fruit of incipient consumerism, and, partly as a result of their dramatic internal migration, witnessed the structural transformation of their households and communities. Grandchildren of the Revolution, they reaped the benefits of an earlier generation's conflict and labor.

As children they heard heroic tales of revolutionary war heroes, the success of a grand constitutional experiment, and the great victory of "the General" at the battle of New Orleans. As young adults they witnessed the construction of one of the great engineering marvels of the nineteenth century, the Erie Canal. And by middle age they had seen their country emerge as a continental giant. For this generation, nothing seemed impossible.

Although some of these men and women were troubled by the inequities associated with class, gender, race, and ethnicity, most were supremely confident in the glorious future of the United States, New York State, and their central position in it.[2] Spurred by a sense of distinctiveness (if not destiny), this generation supported the construction of an immense transportation infrastructure that made markets more accessible, and they both invented and invested in a vast array of agricultural tools that helped revolutionize farm production.

But this is not the story of the "great men" of this era whose contributions helped lead New York from frontier settlement to Empire State. That story has been told before, and told well. Rather, this is a tale of how ordinary farm families in the middle of the nineteenth century embraced social and economic change. This is also the story of the "seduction" of an entire generation. It was these mid-nineteenth-century men and women who, in large numbers, abandoned the security (and drudgery) of yeomanry for the gilt-edged life of material comfort associated with the market economy. Indeed, Tocqueville seemed to have recognized this growing materialism when he noted that for Americans "the little conveniences of life ... [were] uppermost in every mind. No passion ... is more peculiarly ... appropriate to their condition than their love of physical prosperity."[3]

For better or worse, the men and women of this generation embraced consumer materialism. There would be no turning back. The complex market economy inexorably drew both the willing and unwilling into its web. Some actively nurtured this economy by transforming their semi-subsistence farms into more specialized, productive facilities. Others simply reinforced it as willing consumers of cheap cotton cloth, farm implements, or store-bought geegaws. But whether their participation was at the entrepreneurial or consumer level (or both), these farm men and women helped set a new economic course for their state and nation.

This book neither indicts commercial agriculture nor romanticizes the yeoman lifestyle. Rather, it sets out to examine the fundamental transformation of the agricultural economy during the years from the late 1830s up to about 1870 and some of its social implications. The argument is that the rapid spread of the surplus market economy during this period set off a series of profound social, familial, and community changes, the contours of which are probably familiar to most Americans today.

THE CULTURE OF MOBILITY

At the center of these changes was this generation's *culture of mobility*. As the agricultural economy of the nineteenth century developed and as individuals were drawn into it directly or indirectly, millions of New Yorkers used internal migration as either a vehicle of self-improvement or a mechanism for survival. Migration was an important catalyst of change.

The family was the first to change, but not in the way some have assumed. During this period, internal migration was typically associated with the temporary extension of the household rather than its "progressive nucleation" or disruption. The economic and emotional needs of "people in motion" often were met by household members in both the communities of origin and destination. Surplus market farm families in their early married years, for example, often extended their households by providing temporary residence for working kith and kin drawn from an enormous pool of upwardly mobile migrants. This strategy was a common one and reveals an important human capital component of successful surplus market involvement.

The dramatic migration of mid-nineteenth-century New Yorkers in the context of this changing economy also helped transform the social structure and composition of rural communities. Areas that offered commercial opportunities were transformed by migrants into dynamic boomtowns with rapid population growth. Other communities experienced the problems and possibilities associated with depopulation. Still others matured into stable communities with high persistence, low in-migration, and significant intergenerational transfer of wealth. Analysis of these distinctive demographic and economic patterns provides some important insights into the uneven process of agricultural change during the middle of the nineteenth century.[4]

THE MARKET INVOLVEMENT DEBATE

But how do we interpret these fundamental social and economic changes? This central question has interested historians for decades.

Writing during the consensus-oriented 1950s, scholars such as Louis Hartz, Daniel Boorstin, Richard Hofstadter, and a host of others focused on what they saw as the defining characteristic of nineteenth-century rural people—an eager acceptance of capitalism. During the 1950s, scholars often saw commercial agriculture as one of America's most dramatic triumphs at a time when national triumphs were expected. The immense productivity of American farmers during the twentieth century was seen as evidence of an economic system that worked extremely well. For these scholars, commercial agriculture had always been widespread, and American farmers in the past typically were seen as highly individualistic market producers.[5]

Beginning in the late 1970s, however, this debate was restructured by scholars working in the "new rural history." Cognizant of persistent problems in the American economy and influenced by a growing body of research that demonstrated the importance of traditional values in economic change, these scholars argued that market production of the mid-nineteenth century often was tempered by values associated with the family, kin relationships, and the community. While these scholars have not settled this debate, they have provided us with an important counterpoint to the pervasive though sometimes tacit idea that the exclusive goal of all farmers in the past was to make money. As one scholar recently put it, "profit maximizing *homo economicus* has not been the only actor on the stage of history." More recently, Winifred Rothenberg and other scholars have shown that the market economy emerged sometime in the mid-eighteenth century, with poor subsistence farmers participating to feed their families and wealthy commercial farmers selling a surplus on the open market for cash. In short, the market economy emerged in this country when transactional costs declined and when legal protection of contracts and private property became widespread.[6]

This book builds on each of these historiographical perspectives. Clearly, there was widespread (although in many cases occasional) market participation from at least the middle of the eighteenth century. However, it was not until the mid-nineteenth century that most farmers had become oriented toward surplus market production. But while surplus production was becoming an important goal, many farmers maintained traditional production methods and household relationships. In addition to their nominal investment in agricultural tools and land, for example, many surplus market farmers of this period used their available human capital to improve their yields and achieve their surplus. For these farmers, the shift toward commercial agricultural was structured as much by kinship and tradition as it was by the drive for profit.

A NEW GENERATION OF CONSUMERS

Although most mid-nineteenth-century New York farmers seemed determined to maintain their traditional values, few saw the hardships, continual labor, and austere lifestyle of semi-subsistence yeomanry as a virtue. Indeed, by mid-nineteenth century a growing number had become fascinated with the possibility of owning a new wall clock, a "store-bought" dress, a buggy, paint and varnish for the house, or simply some cloth or buttons. Thus, while many of these farmers may not have been concerned initially about profit maximization, scientific agriculture, or the emerging business world, they were excited about cheap consumer goods. For these farm families, the agricultural transition was nurtured in large part by the emerging material/consumer culture of the mid-nineteenth century.

Once again, it was the farmers of the mid-nineteenth century who were at the cutting edge of these dramatic changes. Their field crops, dairy products, and other agricultural produce found ready markets in the burgeoning urban centers along the eastern seaboard, river valleys, and canal corridors. Moreover, the growing demand for food during this period raised the price of many agricultural commodities, sometimes substantially.

For example, the price of winter wheat on the New York market increased by about 50 percent between 1840 and 1860, and corn and hog prices skyrocketed nearly 70 percent during the same period. From 1843 (the low point of the post-1837 deflation) to 1861 (the last year before the Civil War hyperinflation), farm crop prices increased 33.9 percent while farm "derivative" prices increased by 40.9 percent. Those of industrial products available to consumers, on the other hand, remained virtually unchanged. Moreover, during this same period, the price index of all commodities increased by only 16.9 percent. In short, farm prices increased at about twice the rate of all other consumer products during this period.[7]

This situation could be seductive. A farm family could sell its surplus later to be known as a cash crop, at what must have appeared to be an ever-increasing price. And with these profits they could purchase cheap consumer goods and farm items from cotton cloth to iron plows. In fact, it is no exaggeration to argue that the mid-nineteenth-century farmer fueled America's first Industrial Revolution. As Fred Bateman has noted, "most goods manufactured in the antebellum economy depended heavily on rural buyers. ... In every region ... manufacturers ... sold a substantial portion of their goods to farmers."[8]

For many in this fortunate generation, everything seemed to fall into place. The insidious Irish potato blight, for example, devastated that country, sending millions to their graves and perhaps an equal number to the cities of North America. However, this tragedy also helped create large urban markets for a variety of products ranging from wheat, potatoes, and hay to livestock, dairy products, and maple syrup. Similarly, the Crimean War provided opportunities for some New York farmers to export their grain to civilian and military populations alike in Europe. Moreover, the discovery of gold at Sutter's Mill in Sacramento, California, in the late 1840s eventually pumped $2 million of the precious metal into the U.S. economy and further inflated the prices of agricultural commodities during the 1850s. And finally, our bloody Civil War, while devastating an entire generation of young Americans, passed by many mid-nineteenth-century New York farmers who often were too old to fight but still young enough to reap the enormous economic rewards of wartime markets.

RISING EXPECTATIONS

For a substantial proportion of these men and women, *this* was the golden age of agriculture. As a result, many slowly abandoned the austerity of semi-subsistence yeomanry for the greater material wealth associated with surplus market production. Clearly, the bridge between nonsurplus yeomanry and surplus market production was not simply the drive for profit but also a growing demand for cheap consumer goods that made life a little nicer and a little easier. As Tamara Hareven has noted in another context, "New consumption patterns can lead to changes in values."[9] In this sense, the "new" values associated with the marketplace slowly were nurtured by a growing materialism and a distinctive shift in consumption patterns.

Many yeomen, producing below surplus initially, had no intention of transforming either their production or their lifestyle to enter the commercial marketplace. But as industrialization made more and more consumer goods available to them, their materialism and attendant rising expectations drew them into surplus market production. By slowly adopting the material basis of the marketplace, these farmers were able to maintain traditional values of family and community while reaping the benefits of the new economic order. Indeed, many of these people were not *Homo economicus* but just ordinary *Homo sapiens* attracted to the "good life" that the marketplace seemed to offer.

In a "simpler," certainly less-materialistic, time at the beginning of the nineteenth century, the typical New York farmer's household inventory was quite modest. In fact, for about fifty dollars a farm family could provide for all their material needs. Their hand-built homes were seldom painted, and carpets or luxury items such as grandfather clocks rarely were found outside the merchant class.

With the advent of manufacturing in the factory setting, however, this situation changed. During the middle of the nineteenth century, we can see a dramatic increase in both the volume and availability of manufactured consumer goods and a corresponding decline in their prices. Between 1849 and 1869, for example, the number of manufacturing establishments in the United States more than doubled while value added by manufacturing tripled. Similarly, the number of manufacturing employees jumped 115 percent during this same period. As early as 1850, New York had 23,553 manufacturing establishments, nearly $1 million invested, and an annual product of almost a quarter of a billion dollars.[10]

As a result, a bewildering array of cheap household consumer goods was becoming available to New York farmers. The grandfather clock of the early nineteenth century cost about $60 (more than the combined household inventory of most farm families of that era), but wooden wall clocks manufactured by Eli Terry and others in the Connecticut Valley were being sold by country peddlers and village merchants for as little as $3 by mid-century. Other items that were out of reach for many farmers in the early nineteenth century had by 1850 become affordable and commonplace. A wool mattress that cost $50 in 1811, for example, was soon replaced by one made of cotton for $35. Its price rapidly declined to $12.50 in the 1830s, and it cost a mere $5 by the 1850s. Similarly, a silver watch, an expensive gift item in the early part of the century, was only $16 in the late 1820s and by 1860 cost less than $7. A brass watch was even less expensive at about $5. And a ten-plate stove, which cost $20 at the beginning of the century, was less than $10 by the 1850s.[11]

These statistics demonstrate clearly both the increased production and falling prices of various manufactured commodities, but historians have found it more difficult to document the consumption of these goods by Americans. This is because of the paucity of data that demonstrate consumption and a historiographical tradition that dates the emergence of the consumer society in the United States from the late nineteenth and early twentieth centuries. In recent years, however, a number of historians, using new sources and techniques, have demonstrated that there was something of a "consumer revolution" as early as the eighteenth century. Lois Greene Carr and Lorena Walsh, for example, have used probate inventories to examine this question and found clear evidence of "consumerism" in colonial Chesapeake Bay society.[12]

More recently, Elizabeth Perkins has used probate records and store accounts to investigate the consumption practices of late-eighteenth- and early-nineteenth-century Kentucky settlers. She found that in roughly a twenty-five-year period, 1781–83 to 1801–4, the proportion of probate inventories that mentioned rather basic consumer items increased significantly. The percentage of those that listed glassware, for example, increased from 11 percent in the early period to 52 percent twenty years later. During that same period, those listing chairs jumped from only 25 to 63 percent, those listing tables from 25 to 61 percent, and those listing mattresses climbed from 54 to 80 percent. Clearly, Perkins has demonstrated a sharp increase in consumerism by the beginning of the nineteenth century in at least one American community.[13]

David Jaffee also has emphasized the growth of consumerism during these years by focusing on the important role of the "mobile merchant" as a "peddler of progress." For example, Jaffee notes that in 1841 there were only 302 peddlers licensed by the state of New York, but fifteen years later in 1855, that number had soared to 4,131. The increase for the country as a whole during these years also was substantial. In fact, for Jaffee: "Peddlers were central to the process of creating a new culture—a market culture in the antebellum North. They brought that culture in the form of goods to rural people."[14]

Thus by the beginning of the nineteenth century and perhaps earlier, a substantial proportion of Americans, in both cities and the countryside, were purchasing consumer goods. In fact, many observers of the time had begun to recognize an incipient materialism among Americans. As mentioned above, Tocqueville wrote that "the desire of acquiring the comforts of the world haunts the imagination ... their minds ... intoxicated by ... small enjoyments."[15] And he singled out the American farmer as having acquired a penchant "for physical gratifications."[16] Once he begins "to enjoy these pleasures ... he is eager to increase his means of satisfying these tastes more completely."[17]

Moreover, many farmers were becoming cognizant of their own growing materialism. For example, Benjamin Gue, a mid-nineteenth-century farmer from upstate New York, left us a number of detailed diaries that provide rare glimpses into the everyday consumption practices of farmers during this period. His entry for August 21, 1851, noted that after "sowing grass seed" and plowing he "took Sara Ann to Palmyra on a trading expedition. We got there about 1:00 and staid until about 3 in the meantime Sarah Ann bought a new dress, a carpet—30 yards—cost $21.25, [and] a looking glass, a bureau and a settee, the whole of which cost $18 1/2. After buying a lot of trumpery, we went home."[18]

Other entries throughout his diaries suggest that the purchases of both "trumpery" and haberdashery were common. On Tuesday, November 8, 1848, for example, he recorded a trip to Rochester to buy a horse, but also "got a hat." Similarly, on Thursday the 10th he noted that he "bought 16 dollars worth of clothes and five dollars worth of books."[19]

The account books of William Van Orden also provide us with some insights into the buying habits of one New York commercial farmer during this period. In April and May of 1860, for example, William recorded twenty-four days of expenditures, ten of which involved consumer items, as opposed to food or materials for the farm. These included "a lot of furniture and crockery" for $48 on April 2 and a "pair of slippers" for $.50 on April 12. Then on May 1 he bought "shoes, self and children" for $4.86 and the next day a chair for $3. On the 6th of May he bought "stockings—$2.50," and on the 15th he bought "curtains at $3" and also had his watch repaired for $2. Finally, on May 23 and 31, he made two purchases for "wife"—a skirt worth $1.63 and lace for $.69.[20]

Finally, Isaac Phillips Roberts, the first dean of the College of Agriculture at Cornell University, recalled in his *Autobiography of a Farm Boy* the dramatic growth in consumerism during his life (he was born in 1833). He noted how in one generation New Yorkers "changed from homespun clothes, coonskin caps and shoes made from boot tops, to ... patent leather shoes ... long frock coats and silk hats."[21]

These examples suggest that by the middle of the nineteenth century many New York farmers were being attracted to the simple material comforts of the new economic order. As Tocqueville noted, their "taste for physical gratification ... was rather modest ... their goal was [to make] life more comfortable and convenient." But as this observer warned, "[though] these are small objects ... the soul clings to them, it dwells upon them closely ... till they at last shut out the rest of the world."[22]

EQUIPMENT AND HUMAN CAPITAL

To take advantage of these new consumer opportunities, many New York farmers of this period began to reconsider their traditional ideas concerning investment in both equipment and human capital. This led slowly to a greater acceptance of agricultural tools as well as a keener understanding of both the importance and costs of human capital on the farmstead. In turn, this new mind-set helped nurture the surplus market economy of the mid-nineteenth century.

During these years, hired agricultural labor had become scarce and more expensive. Many potential farmworkers had sought riches in the goldfields of California or were attracted to cheaper lands in the West made accessible through military land bounties, the pre-emption laws of the 1830s and 1840s, the sale of railroad land in the 1850s, and the land acts of the early 1860s. Others simply moved a few miles to the next county with the hope of purchasing a farm of their own. Moreover, with the onset of the Civil War in 1861, thousands of young men traded their spades for rifles. For all these reasons, the supply of hired agricultural laborers had been depleted dramatically, and wages inched upward.[23]

Similarly, many New York farm sons already had begun to move from the country to the city, depleting the pool of domestic farmworkers. The agricultural press continually lamented the fact that many of their brightest young men were leaving the farm for the "glitter of the city." The January 1857 issue of *The Northern Farmer,* for example, noted "who does not know that multitudes of farmers' sons every year leave the old homestead in the country to seek their fortunes in villages and cities."[24]

As a result of this growing labor shortage, some farmers restructured their households to improve their basic human capital and ultimately their overall yields, while others invested in many of the agricultural tools and implements that had become available. Perhaps they read of a new plow or reaper in one of the many agricultural journals that began publication during this period such as *The Cultivator, The Ploughboy, The Northern Farmer,* or *The Genesee Farmer.* Or perhaps they witnessed a field trial of one of these machines at their county or state fair.[25]

Whatever the source of information, this generation of New York farmers was in a financial position by the middle of the century to purchase the new seed sowers, mowers, plows, farm wagons, churns, and cheese presses. Born in the first decades of the nineteenth century, these men and women were in their most financially secure years by midcentury, at the very time when agricultural prices had increased substantially. The purchase of, say, $200 of farm tools could help them become more competitive by increasing their productivity and overall yields.

But what could a farmer purchase for $200 during this period? William Van Orden, once again, has provided us with some answers to that question in his account books beginning in March 1859 when he bought his farm. In addition to livestock, "sundries," Peruvian guano, and food, Van Orden purchased an assortment of agricultural "tools" and related items to establish his farm. These included an ox yoke for $2.62, a farm wagon for $62, a box of wagon grease at $.25, a wagon jack for $2, a pair of oxbows for $.50, a whip for $4.56, a pair of horse blankets for $2.25, a cultivator for $10, a neck yoke for $1.50, a "light on-business wagon" for $105, locks for $.75, and a set of double harnesses for $34. These items were typical of some of the "start-up" purchases a farmer might make during this period. The Van Orden account books as well as other sorts of quantitative and qualitative evidence suggest that nominal investments in agricultural tools had become rather commonplace among mid-nineteenth-century New York farmers.[26]

EUPHORIA AND BITTERNESS

But before mid-nineteenth-century New York farmers were able to reap the benefits of this fundamental economic transformation, many experienced the euphoria and bitterness of the boom-bust agricultural economy, especially the critical 1830s and early 1840s. These lessons then were reinforced two decades later in the panic of 1857. Taken together, these booms and busts represented a critical turning point of the mid-nineteenth-century agricultural transition.

During the early 1830s, real estate values soared in the Empire State, drawing many farmers headlong into the euphoria of quick profits from land speculation. Between 1830 and 1836, for example, real estate prices in New York State rose 50 to 150 percent, while bank loans across the country doubled from $28 million to $56 million. The great land boom had begun. Then suddenly in 1837 the boom ended and the nation plunged into an insidious deflationary spiral. But as is often the case, economic collapse helped promote change. The boom-bust of the late 1830s and early 1840s, and to a lesser degree the cyclical downturn in 1857, seemed to have triggered a widespread shift in attitudes toward farming that in turn helped transform the agricultural economy for the rest of the nineteenth century.[27]

The inflation of 1830–36 was broken unmercifully in the panic of 1837 and was followed by a monetary deflation of nearly four years that exploded the land investment boom of the previous decade. The deflationary crash, of course, secured profits for bankers and other creditors who were now guaranteed repayment of their outstanding loans with deflated dollars or the homestead itself.

However, the sudden fall in prices brought chaos to farmers in three ways. First, the price of their land plummeted, offering little possibility of selling the farm for a profit in a season or two. Second, the prices of agricultural commodities fell sharply following 1837, providing little cash profit to pay off existing farm mortgages much less to buy the geegaws of the itinerant peddler or local shopkeeper. And finally, lower prices meant that there would be no "inflation relief" from debts. Although the 50 percent inflation of these years had meant that short-term, fixed-rate loans were much "easier" to pay off with inflated dollars, the full deflated payment regime had now returned with a vengeance. The result was that thousands of overextended farmers were unable to contend with this financial nightmare and lost their land. Some were forced into tenancy, while others simply left farming to try their luck in cities such as Albany, Rochester, Syracuse, or Buffalo.[28]

The financial devastation caused by the panic of 1837 had a lasting impact on many farmers. Some, like William Buckminister, responded to it by calling for a return to the security of semi-subsistence yeomanry. Appalled by the collapse of the economy, he warned readers of *The Genesee Farmer* in 1838: "Though we cannot afford to raise grain to carry to markets neither can we afford to resort to our seaports to buy it. ... By raising our own grain we avoid [this dilemma]. Hence the maxim that farmers should live principally on their own production."[29]

Few heeded Buckminister's "maxim," but the memories of this

economic nightmare lingered throughout this period and had a significant though ironic effect. The collapse of the agricultural economy and
the financial ruin of thousands of farmers set the stage for a dramatic
agricultural transition. For the next three decades, New York farmers
reversed more than a century of wasteful farming methods and embraced a new era of land nurture. Rather than perceiving land *solely* as
a disposable commodity, which had been typical as late as the 1830s,
many farmers had begun to recognize that the real value of their land
was not in its resale but in the commercial crops that could be produced
on it. As John Falconer put it, by the beginning of the 1840s "the age
of farming by extension of area had ceased and that by increased investment of capital had well begun." The ancient method of the "summer fallow" was gradually abandoned, and by mid-century, "scientific
farming" and the "new horticulture" had become more widespread.[30]

THE AGRICULTURAL PRESS

While economic collapse had a sobering effect on New York farmers, the emerging agricultural press spread the new gospel of intensive
land use. As Whitney Cross has noted, by mid-century, journals such as
The Genesee Farmer and *The Cultivator* "probably circulated more
thoroughly among the rural folk of Western New York than any other
paper."[31] In fact, most of the important New York agricultural journals
of the nineteenth century began publication during this period. These
included *The Genesee Farmer* (1831), *The Cultivator* (1834), *The Wool
Grower and Magazine of Agriculture and Horticulture* (1849), *Country
Gentleman* (1859), *The Northern Farmer* (1845), and *The Working
Farmer* (1849), to name just a few.[32]

The advice to farmers printed in these journals was sometimes
misguided, and journals occasionally promoted get-rich-quick schemes
like the well-known silk worm craze. Nevertheless, it is difficult to
overstate the importance of these and dozens of other less successful
journals published during this period in promoting and communicating
the ideas of the "new agriculture."[33]

The rural editors of these important new agricultural journals not
only displayed an undaunted confidence in the importance of the new

scientific farming but also were excited about the central role that the new farmer would play in the future of America. An early issue of *The Cultivator*, for example, noted with confidence, "Alongside the [rail]roads, whose iron bands unite our most distant cities, upon banks of rivers and canals, whose waters bear away the products of our soil, there have been springing up, intelligent thinking farmers."[34]

Indeed, "intelligent thinking farmers" were springing up everywhere, and the passion for scientific agriculture seemed to consume more and more farmers each day. A frequent contributor to *The Cultivator* known as H.C.W. from Putnam Valley, New York, reflected this very well: "Depend on it, science and agriculture must go hand in hand. ... Free yourself from those prejudices against book farming ... and it will not be long before your calling ... will rise to its true height."[35] Even while working in his field, the new "scientific" farmer was consumed by a sense of rationality: "While he holds the plow with his hands, his head is at work; he thinks, he plans, the hours fly swiftly away for his mind is working as well as his body."[36]

Of course, for Luther Tucker of *The Cultivator*, T.B. Minor of *The Northern Farmer*, and dozens of other mid-nineteenth-century rural editors, the agricultural press was responsible for this great transformation to rationality. A speech reprinted in the 1848 issue of *The Cultivator* expressed this sentiment well: "Slowly, silently, almost by stealth, without the knowledge of the man himself this mighty engine undermines old prejudices and teaches the farmer that however independent he may be he is not so that the experience of others will not profit him. ... We are becoming more like liberal ... aspiring men."[37]

Whatever the cause of this new scientific approach to agriculture, the editors were right about one thing: it had begun to undermine old prejudices and was creating a class of "liberal, aspiring men" who, with their families, would extend the surplus market economy from its traditional pockets located around New York City and the eastern river valleys to the rest of the state.

* * *

In the pages that follow we will examine the lives of several thousand everyday New Yorkers of the mid-nineteenth century to explore the relationship between population movement and economic change. In the next chapter, we begin our examination of the central role of migration. We will discover that migration helped mid-nineteenth-century farm households make the most of their commercial opportunities while at the same time allowing them to maintain traditional patterns of production and their commitments to both family and kin. First we assess the significance of the "mobility transition" that appears to have begun in the second quarter of the nineteenth century. We will see that within a single generation the volume of internal migration in America nearly doubled. We then examine both the demographic and economic characteristics of migrants in the past and explore interpretations of how migration may have affected their attitudes and behaviors. In short, we will examine the importance of migration in reallocating human capital and in providing both the entrepreneurial leadership and consumer culture that nurtured economic change.

But if migration was central to the transformation of the agricultural economy of the nineteenth century, why have scholars, until recently, ignored its role? In Chapter 3 we explore this question by examining how historians, sociologists, and others typically have seen migrants as either purveyors of social disruption or victims of economic change but seldom as central actors in the unfolding historical drama. This misunderstanding of migration as a general historical process has been compounded by a stubborn pastoral myth rooted in a collective sense of loss of gemeinschaft during the nineteenth century. As a result, rural people in the past are seen as virtually immobile when compared with their urban counterparts. The pastoral myth moreover has been reinforced by methodological problems in the measurement of internal migration, notably the "residual issue" associated with nominal record linkage.[38]

Thus, the powerful stereotypes of a stable, bucolic countryside sharply contrasted with the transient, rootless city have been grist for many political mills in the past but, alas, have not been very good history. In fact, the countryside was in constant motion, with some rural communities actually more migratory than many urban ones. Tocqueville may have been right all along when he said, "A farmer builds his house but lets someone else put the roof on, he plows his field but allows another to bring in the harvest so that he might carry his changeable longings elsewhere."[39]

With this new perspective, we turn our attention to the agricultural economy of the mid-nineteenth century, which we explore in detail in Chapters 4 and 5. The methodological basis of these chapters is the measurement of net yields in 1855 and 1865 New York State. Agricultural production first was converted into a common caloric equivalent and then adjusted by livestock and human consumption needs. This provided a net yield estimate for each sampled farm household.[40] From this, farmers who were producing a surplus for market and those who were not could be identified.

Analysis of these data demonstrate that although most farmers in mid-nineteenth-century New York had some market involvement, just more than half produced a surplus in 1855. By the end of the decade, however, two out of three New York farmers had produced a marketable surplus. This decade, culminating in the Civil War, appears to be an important watershed in New York agricultural history. Not only were most farmers producing a surplus by 1865, but their burgeoning net yields allowed greater specialization in the nonagricultural sector of the economy and sustained growth throughout the Empire State. The mid-nineteenth-century agricultural transition then helped fuel America's second Industrial Revolution.

Nevertheless, many farm households at the beginning of this decade were unable to meet their own nutritional needs, much less produce a surplus for market. As a result, these farmers employed a variety of production and barter strategies to survive. Chapter 4 focuses on these households and examines their diaries, population, and agricultural production records as well as the newspapers and literature they read to reveal a rich tapestry of rural life based on family, kin, and community work relationships and slowly evolving definitions of gender roles.

In Chapter 5 we turn our attention to surplus market producers. Insights from their diaries, account books, local newspapers, official records, the agricultural press, as well as the manuscript agricultural and population census present a portrait of the surplus market farm household. This is somewhat different from that of the "harried businessman" popularized several decades ago in the historical literature. But it also does not conform to the precapitalist subsistence cultivator who rejected the market economy as irrelevant. Rather, we find that the surplus market farmer of the mid-nineteenth century was a curious mixture of persistent traditional values associated with family and community integrated with a growing sense of individualism nurtured by rising expectations of a better life through market involvement. Although surplus market farmers were similar in some ways to their yeoman neighbors, they also were very different. Their investment strategies, migration profiles, household structures, gender relationships, fertility (the number of children born to each woman), work strategies, and growing wealth all were clear indications of those differences. As we will see, these differences would become more dramatic during this decade.

These changes, of course, were not uniform throughout the Empire State. Not only were there distinct differences in the strategies used by individual farm households to achieve a surplus, but the nature of the surplus market economy also varied significantly across New York. By examining the link between migration and economic change at the community level, we can see the important relationship between patterns of population movement, market access, historical development, and the level of commercial involvement. In Chapter 6 we will explore these complex relationships.

By examining the emergence of these unique market ecologies, we can document critical variations in rural economic change. In some areas we can see the early signs of agricultural consolidation and a growing stratification of farm values; in others we see unprecedented economic growth offering abundant opportunities for aggressive in-migrants. And in still others we can observe the gradual emergence of an incipient commercial economy. In short, by examining each of these market ecologies we can begin to appreciate the complexity of the mid-nineteenth-century agricultural transition and its attendant shifts in population movement, wealth concentration, and production.

While the efficient reallocation of human capital through migration helped fuel the tremendous growth of New York's agricultural economy during the mid-nineteenth century, it also provided the opportunity for thousands of farm households with limited resources to engage in surplus market production. This is the focus of Chapter 7. Although many aspiring market farm households lacked the wealth and materials necessary to enter the surplus marketplace, they often had hidden resources of a different sort: human capital derived from the large numbers of migrating kith and kin who were streaming across the state. These mobile men and women were a central component of New York's culture of mobility, although they have remained virtually invisible because of their temporary position in households and communities in the past. For years, students of migration have speculated about the role played by these "invisible migrants," but as a result of seemingly insurmountable measurement problems, these migrants have remained little more than a historical curiosity. However, by using continuous-years-of-residence data recorded for each household member in the 1855 New York State Census, these invisible migrants slowly have begun to materialize. With these data we can trace the in-migration paths of relatives and boarders into both stable and migrating households by comparing their continuous-years-of-residence with those of other household members.

We see that many farmers in mid-nineteenth-century New York State (and presumably elsewhere in the North at this time) faced a dilemma: They were drawn to the material consumer culture of the market economy, but they lacked the capital to enter it. Moreover, their growing taste for material goods had awakened their sense of individualism associated with profit, but at the same time they clung tenaciously to the traditions of the past. The solution for many was to increase their yields while maintaining traditional forms of production and kin relations by extending their households with migrating relatives, friends, and strangers from other communities.

Cautious of the enthusiastic rhetoric of rural editors heralding the dawn of a new age of agriculture were thousands of farm households that used these strategies to produce a surplus crop. Indeed, many of these farmers were very clever. They knew what it took to squeeze a surplus from worn-out soil. They understood the emerging market structure and the role of regional specialization within it. But they also had financial limitations as well as familial traditions and production

strategies that they were unwilling to abandon. While many were fascinated, and sometimes bemused, by the plethora of new gadgets, implements, and farm machines that were being demonstrated in local
field trials and at county and state fairs, many continued to use older,
more familiar tools and employ less-innovative methods of cultivation
and harvesting that would satisfy both traditional family commitments
and financial considerations.[41]

Many commercial farm families at mid-century, for example, continued to employ collective household labor strategies to harvest grain,
while others maintained family-oriented activities such as maple syrup
harvesting even in the face of clear evidence that its production was not
very profitable. The Porter Blisses, who will be discussed further in
Chapter 3, were quite successful commercial farmers, but Porter often
wrote of "cradling oats" with his father at harvest and thrashing grain
by hand as a communal activity. The Blisses also maintained traditional
labor relationships and bartering strategies in tandem with successful
surplus market involvement. Similarly, the Jonah Ransoms of rural
Greene County made the difficult transition to the surplus market economy between 1855 and 1865 with very little investment in agricultural
tools, no horses for plowing, and no purchased fertilizers for soil enrichment. Their strategy was to board three young, male, migrant relatives to help them increase their yields. In this way, the Ransoms were
able to enter the surplus market economy more obliquely—not through
capital investments but through kin cooperation and a great deal of hard
work.

Others slowly abandoned field crop production and moved into
dairying and wool production, perhaps as much for cultural as for economic reasons. These activities were more labor intensive than field
crop cultivation, and yields could be increased more easily by expanding the size of the working household rather than investing in agricultural implements. Moreover, these activities satisfied both the desire to
maintain traditional family-oriented production patterns and the desire
to earn a profit through surplus market involvement.

The success of the Blisses and thousands of others like them was
achieved by wedding a bit of the "new" agriculture, such as an iron
plow, a cornsheller, and a wagon, with more traditional agricultural

methods. The Jonah Ransoms, on the other hand, unable to purchase more land, and perhaps unwilling to alter fundamentally their traditional production patterns, bolstered their agricultural output by temporarily extending their household with three migrant relatives and moving vigorously into dairying and wool production. Like many other New York farmers of this period, they recognized the importance of migrating kin as potential workers. These aggressive, often upwardly mobile men and women represented a key, though sometimes invisible, element of New York's culture of mobility that helped farmers of limited means and sometimes traditional ideas to push, shove, and struggle into the new surplus market economy.

Mobile Americans made their mark as they moved across, settled in, and eventually cultivated the wilderness.

CHAPTER 2

The Countryside in Motion

The fundamental shift in attitudes toward production and the rising material expectations of rural upstate New Yorkers at mid-nineteenth century were tied directly to important demographic changes. In addition to a decline in both fertility and mortality, one of the most significant of these changes was an increase in internal migration. Of course, people had always moved in response to natural disasters, climatic changes, political repression, or war. But over the years the tempo of migration had increased, and by mid-century it had become a powerful though often misunderstood demographic change.

During the nineteenth century, hundreds of Europeans had traveled extensively throughout America, recording their impressions of this young nation. Some were fascinated by its political institutions, others appalled by its popular culture. But most were baffled by a sense of impermanence that seemed to have pervaded all levels of this society.

A STRANGE UNREST

In 1839, for example, Michael Chevalier, a French official inspecting the public works of this country, remarked that Americans had "no root in the soil; [and] were always disposed to emigrate." He concluded that an American "is devoured with a passion for locomotion [and] cannot stay in one place ... he must go and come, he must stretch his limbs and keep his muscles in play."[1]

Chevalier's notable contemporary, Alexis de Tocqueville, also pondered this restlessness, remarking that Americans "daily quit the spots whic⊦ gave them birth, to acquire ... domains in a remote region."[2] Tocqueville felt this "strange unrest" and "restless disposition" were "distinctive" traits of Americans.[3]

What Tocqueville saw so clearly, yet was unable to explain fully, was a fundamental change in the volume and patterns of migration among Americans. In Tocqueville's more familiar "aristocratic"[4] world, "families remain for centuries in the same condition, often on the same spot ... man almost always knows his ancestors ... [and] thinks he sees his remote descendents."[5] In short, the contours of this world were relatively constant, though subject to the natural rhythms of life.

By the time of Tocqueville's grand American tour, however, the basic demographic parameters of American life were changing rapidly. Migration had become a central feature of the "equation of life," altering virtually every aspect of the social environment. America was being transformed fundamentally by the process of migration.

Of course, the endless cycle of life would continue to shape the social and economic existence of mid-nineteenth-century men and women. But now migration interacted with these natural rhythms to change their world forever. The community had become a temporary place in a rapidly changing social drama. Moreover, permanence, the hallmark of traditional society, had been replaced by a rapid procession of people, institutions, and ideas, all carried by America's extraordinary culture of mobility.

THE MOBILITY TRANSITION

Although most of us recognize the rapid pace of population mobility today, scholars have had some difficulty documenting levels of migration over time. This is because we have very little migration data from the past. One of the most important sources of migration data available to American historians is the U.S. Census, beginning in 1850. In that year federal census enumerators were instructed to record the names and birthplaces of each individual in the household. These data have provided us with important information on the lifetime interstate and international migration of mid-nineteenth-century Americans. As the U.S. Census became more comprehensive in the decades following 1850, additional information concerning both the in- and out-migration of Americans became available. Today, social scientists have a wealth of data to use in comparing migration profiles of individuals and groups across time and space.

To examine interstate migration before 1850 or intercounty migration anytime during (or before) the nineteenth century, however, historians have had to be more creative and work much harder. The most important method we have developed to estimate these sorts of migration is the so-called persistence rate. This rate measures the proportion of an initial population that remained in a community over a period of time, usually ten years. Its inverse (100 minus the persistence rate) is a fair estimate of the volume of out-migration from a community, subject to some adjustments, notably mortality. Historians typically take two comparable populations lists (such as two complete census manuscripts or city directories) from two time periods and then "link" or trace individuals between them. The number of individuals successfully linked becomes the numerator of the rate, and the initial population (at risk to migrate) becomes the denominator. The biases inherent in the technique of "nominal record linkage" (see Chapter 3) are well known and tend to overstate the degree of population turnover, especially in cities. Nevertheless, a careful linking methodology by hand, machine, or both can yield important estimates of out-migration.[6]

In order to examine changes in the volume of migration in the past, persistence rates from more than one hundred communities were collected for this study. The inverses of these persistence rates then were plotted for conceptual clarity to reveal the percentage of a community's initial population that presumably out-migrated each decade. By examining Figure 2.1 we can see a distinct increase in levels of out-migration by mid-nineteenth century.

Between 1800 and 1840 the mean percentage of out-migrants (nonpersisters) from their communities each decade ranged from 48 to 56 percent, with a average of about 55 percent. After mid-century, however, all these out-migration rates (nonpersistence) were greater than 50 percent, with a high of more than 67 percent and an average of about 65 percent. This represents a significant increase in migration.

However, we must address a number of issues concerning these

FIGURE 2.1
Nineteenth-Century Migration

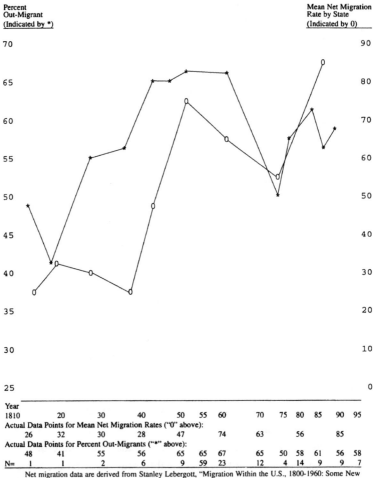

Percent
Out-Migrant
(Indicated by *)

Mean Net Migration
Rate by State
(Indicated by 0)

Year 1810	20	30	40	50	55	60	70	75	80	85	90	95
Actual Data Points for Mean Net Migration Rates ("0" above):												
26	32	30	28	47		74	63		56		85	
Actual Data Points for Percent Out-Migrants ("*" above):												
48	41	55	56	65	65	67	65	50	58	61	56	58
N= 1	1	2	6	9	59	23	12	4	14	9	9	7

Net migration data are derived from Stanley Lebergott, "Migration Within the U.S., 1800-1960: Some New Estimates," *Journal of Economic History* 30(1970):839-846. The mean absolute values of net migration were plotted for New England, Middle Atlantic, and East North Central states for comparability during the nineteenth century. See Table 2, p. 846. Figures refer to the mean number of net migrants per 1000 residents estimated from the mid-decade population of states.

Out-migration estimates are based on data derived from the extant persistence literature. For the sake of conceptual clarity, the inverse of the persistence rate was plotted (100 – persistence rate). Sources of persistence rates are as follows and can be found in the bibliography: Alcorn, "Leadership and Stability"; Barrows, "Hurryin' Hoosiers"; Bogue, *From Prairie to Cornbelt; Bowers "Crawford Township"*; Cogswell, *Tenure, Activity and Age*; Coleman, *"Restless Grant County"*; Curti, *The Making of an American Community*; Davenport, "Population Persistence"; Davis, "Prairie Emporium"; Gagan and Mays, "Historical Demography"; Galenson, "Migration and Economic Opportunity"; Griffen, "Workers Divided"; Hopkins, "Occupational and Geographic Mobility"; Katz, *The People of Hamilton*; Kirk and Kirk, "Migration, Mobility"; Knights, *The Plain People of Boston*; Knights and Alcorn, "Most Uncommon Bostonians"; Lantz and Alix, "Occupational Mobility"; Malin, "The Turnover of Farm Population"; Mann, "The Decade after the Gold Rush"; Parkerson, "How Mobile?"; Ralston, "Migration and Settlement"; Robbins, "Opportunity and Persistence"; Taylor, *Liberty Men*; Thernstrom, *Poverty and Progress*; and Thernstrom and Knights, "Men in Motion."

data before we continue. The first is that scholars have not examined many communities in the past. For example, there are few estimates of persistence for the early decades of the nineteenth century. Second, and perhaps more important, some of the estimates of population movement in cities may be too high because of problems in nominal record linkage (see Chapter 3). Third, these figures are not adjusted for mortality. Early studies of persistence counted as out-migrants those individuals who had died (the ultimate out-migration). Since these individuals could not be traced (or linked) from one population list to the next, they were mistakenly seen as leaving their communities. Although this is a problem when estimating the true migration for a particular community (it can bias our estimates of out-migration upward by as much as 15 percent), it is less a problem when comparing rates over time. This is because each of the estimates in this series is uncorrected.

Finally, as a number of scholars have argued, the geographic size of the community might affect the persistence rate of a community and distort comparisons between communities. In large geographic communities, such as rural counties, a person might move but not cross the political boundary to become a migrant. In smaller geographic areas, such as cities, a shorter move might result in a migration. On the other hand, rural people typically must move farther to find employment. This issue has been addressed in another context, and it was found that the geographic size of a community was not as important as it appears initially.[7]

Thus, despite these methodological issues, it appears that by the middle of the nineteenth century, the volume of out-migration in North American communities had risen significantly. This of course represented an increase in the residential movement of millions of Americans and suggests that the dramatic social and economic changes experienced by Americans during this period were accompanied by a distinct mobility transition.

Finally, the existence of this mobility transition can also be seen by measures of net migration (see Figure 2.1). With the use of Stanley Lebergott's figures, it was estimated that between 1800 and 1840 there were about thirty net migrants per one thousand individuals, but by 1860 that number had more than doubled to seventy-four per thousand.[8]

In short, this analysis shows that levels of migration increased dramatically during this period and appear to be associated with economic changes in both the industrial and agricultural sectors of the economy during the mid-nineteenth century.

MIGRATION AND TRADITIONAL HISTORIOGRAPHY

The transformation of upstate New York in the decades before 1865 involved more than the emergence of a surplus market economy or even the advent of the consumer society. Ultimately, it meant a physical restructuring of the state itself. Unfortunately, this story has been overlooked or minimized. Traditional accounts of the economic transformation of upstate New York and the rural North in general typically have focused on the entrepreneurs, editors, and statesmen of this era. And make no mistake about it, the invention of new farm implements, the emergence of the agricultural press (see Chapter 5), and the construction of a transportation infrastructure all were critical to the development of the market economy.

But beyond the "great men" was an even greater body of ordinary men and women who purchased the farm tools, read the agricultural journals, and used the canals and railroads to maximize their own economic positions. And more important, at least in this context, these people had a unique willingness to disrupt their lives and migrate again and again to take advantage of new opportunities.

Rather than perceiving political, economic, social, or other external forces as defining exclusively the ultimate destinies of these historical actors, this book examines individual initiative and action. By assuming this perspective, we can see that migration was one of several strategies people used to alter their physical, social, and economic environments. Clearly, although most nineteenth-century Americans had little control over their lives, they could influence their future by moving. And move they did!

THE MID-NINETEENTH-CENTURY MIGRANT

What was the nature of migration during the middle of the nineteenth century? To develop a clearer understanding of this complex process, "continuous years of residence," as recorded in the 1855 New York State Census, was used as a proxy for recent in-migration. This variable then was regressed on a series of independent social and economic factors to determine those that were related to in-migration once all others had been controlled statistically.[9]

This analysis revealed that as an individual aged, he or she became more stable residentially; that native New Yorkers were significantly more stable than other groups; that relatives in the area seemed to root individuals to their community; and that landownership was associated with residential stability. In short, older men and women, native New Yorkers, those living with or near their relatives, and landholders were more likely to have been long-time residents of their communities. On the other hand, younger New Yorkers and those with few family ties and no land tended to be recent in-migrants.

In addition, this analysis demonstrated that there were no significant differences between the in-migration profiles (i.e., continuous years of residence) between urban and rural New Yorkers and those with or without children in the household. Similarly, neither one's occupation nor the value of one's home was related to differences in continuous years of residence. This demonstrates clearly that migration

TABLE 2.1
Regression of Continuous Years of Residence for 1855

Variable	b-value	t-value
German	0.153	−0.02
Married (1 = yes)	−2.555	−1.50
Canadian	0.799	0.12
Professional	3.776	1.09
Children in household (number)	0.300	0.99
British	−0.281	−0.05
Same-surname relatives (living within five dwellings)	7.893	4.45*
Home value	0.000	0.19
Yankee	7.450	1.46
Skilled worker	4.983	1.66
Own land (1 = yes)	12.582	1.95*
Gender (1 = male)	−2.561	−1.21
Age	0.413	8.69*
Laborer	4.133	1.34
Irish	3.967	0.59
Urban (1 = urban)	3.718	0.55
New Yorker	9.051	1.92*
Constant	−13.611	1.97*
R^2 = .346		

Source: 1855 Population Sample (see Appendix 1 for a full description).
*Significant at the .05 level.

was commonplace in New York at this time and transcended many of the basic demographic and economic characteristics of these people. Men and women in rural and urban communities with a variety of occupations and incomes were on the move during the middle of the nineteenth century.

AGE AND MIGRATION

But what does this all mean? First, this study, like most others, demonstrates the important relationship between age and migration. Stated simply, young New Yorkers for a variety of reasons were quite mobile; by middle age many had begun to settle down; and after age fifty-five most were residentially stable. Joseph Smith and Benjamin Gue illustrate some of these patterns. Joseph was nearly forty years old in 1855 and had been a migrant most of his life. Born in Vermont in 1816, he traveled to New York State as a young man, and during his twenties and thirties he migrated numerous times, settling temporarily in communities throughout the state and then moving on. In Genesee County, Joseph met and married his wife Jane. The young couple then traveled to bustling Erie County where they apparently had become moderately successful with Joseph working as a carpenter and farmer. By 1855, however, we find the Smiths living in Caladonia, New York, in northern Livingston County with eleven other members of their household. These included a number of relatives and several boarders.[10]

While Joseph Smith had been a migrant for much of his adult life, Benjamin Gue had persisted in his community until he was in his early thirties when he sought a new life in urban America. After the death of his father in 1851, Benjamin sold his successful farm in Farmington Township, Ontario County, and headed for New York City. In his diary entry of January 1852 he noted: "I ... look back one year ago today I was in farming with a fair prospect of spending many years of my life on our old farm. I well remember how many times I have wished that we could sell out, that I might go and seek my fortune in the world— and now that wish is gratified."[11]

But Ben's stay in New York City was brief. In a short time he had soured on urban life and "came away perfectly cured of all desire to live in a city." Eventually he decided to return to farming, headed west, and apparently used what was left of his inheritance to put a modest down payment on a new farm in Iowa. Thus, although Benjamin had been a long-time persister through his early thirties, he had a brief but furious period of migration and travel, eventually settling in the "West."[12]

Joseph Smith and Ben Gue had very different life histories, but together they illustrate the close relationship between migration and age. Joseph struggled throughout his life, moving dozens of times to try to "make it" in a difficult world. Ben, on the other hand, was much more stable residentially as a young man, but before middle age he exhibited a classic pattern of migration to both the city and the West. Whatever their past migration experiences, by tracing these two men and their families to 1865, we can see that each had settled down in their forties and then remained in their respective communities.

ETHNICITY

This analysis also demonstrates that although native New Yorkers were more likely to have remained in their communities during these years, ethnicity was not related to migration. The major ethnic groups in this sample (Canadian, British, German, and Irish) clearly had both migratory and stable households. In short, immigrants were not necessarily transient, even though many recently had arrived in their communities in 1855. For example, many Irish and German people had recently migrated to cities of upstate New York at mid-century, but when we control this effect by other demographic and economic characteristics, we find that they had migration profiles (i.e., continuous years of residence) similar to those of other residents in their communities of settlement.

These findings contradict a number of stereotypes involving the residential instability of ethnic people in the past.[13] Clearly, their period of continuous years of residence typically was shorter than that of other groups, but this was partly because many of them were very young and had just arrived in New York State. However, like other New Yorkers, as they aged, developed kinship ties in the community, or purchased land, they also became rooted in their communities.

Of course, the recent arrival of thousands of immigrants to New York during this period gave them the appearance of transiency simply because they typically had fewer continuous years of residence in their communities. However, when we trace these same supposedly transient immigrants to the end of the decade, we find that they often remained in their communities of destination.

John O'Brien, originally from Ireland, and Gilbert Jones, from Germany, illustrate this idea. Each arrived in their communities in the early 1850s, and thus each had the appearance of residential transiency using continuous years of residence as our measure of migration. However, when we trace these two young men to the 1865 New York State Census, we find that each had persisted residentially and each apparently had been integrated into the socioeconomic life of their communities. Both men married, both had become U.S. citizens, and both remained residentially stable during this decade despite their appearance of transiency in 1855.[14]

Thus while the measure of continuous years of residence tells us something of an individual's in-migration in 1855, only through forward-tracing nominal record linkage can we determine whether that person persisted residentially. However, even here there are problems. As many scholars have pointed out, some urban ethnic people who appear to have out-migrated might actually have been missed by the researcher in the record-linkage process. This of course reinforces the illusion of ethnic transiency. We know, for example, that historians have had great difficulty linking ethnic people with "common names." Moreover, underenumeration in the U.S. Census, especially in urban areas, tends to exacerbate problems of nominal record linkage.[15] In short, ethnic people in the past often appear to be transient even though many settled down after their initial move to America.

MIGRATION AND THE FAMILY

This analysis also has demonstrated that migration was a family affair. And, as much of the research on migration in the last decade has shown, the so-called Handlin hypothesis can be very misleading.

Nearly forty years ago, in his pioneering study of the immigrant experience, Oscar Handlin argued that the process of immigration had virtually destroyed the family structure of ethnic people.[16] The Handlin hypothesis was applied to immigrants and internal migrants alike for nearly twenty years until historians working in the tradition of the "new social history" began to investigate the role of the family in the migration process using empirical data (see Chapter 7). These scholars demonstrated that although migration was a difficult process, it usually occurred inside and not outside of the household and that as a result it often strengthened familial bonds. (For a more complete discussion of the role of the family in the migration process, see Chapter 7.)

This research builds on the important work of the new social historians. It shows that in mid-nineteenth-century New York, entire families often moved together, with single New Yorkers no more mobile than those who were married. Second, as will be discussed in Chapter 7, supposedly solitary migrants often moved in well-defined "chains" of kin and were supported by their families in receiving communities.

The migration of Emilene Austin and her infant son as well as nineteen-year-old James Burton illustrate the important role of the family in the migration process. The widow Austin at twenty-one appeared to be in serious financial and emotional trouble in 1855. The census revealed that earlier that year Emilene's husband had died, leaving her and an infant son Erland in "dire straights." Perhaps as a result of this personal tragedy, she migrated to Shodack, New York, in Rensselaer County to live with her sister and brother-in-law.[17]

The situation of James Burton, though very different, also underscores the central role of family in migration patterns. James was still in his teens when he left home and moved to rural Sullivan County in April of 1855 to become a farmer's apprentice and boarder in his brother-in-law's household. Although James was still young, his labor would help his adopted family increase their output. Perhaps later he would continue his migration odyssey, which might take him across the county, state, and, perhaps, like Ben Gue, to the far West.[18]

But beyond the immediate household, relatives living nearby also were important in the migration process. As Michael Anderson has noted in his classic study of the family in mid-nineteenth-century Lancashire, kinship did not stop at the front door.[19] In mid-nineteenth-century New York, kin living nearby (same-surname kin living within five dwellings) tended to root individuals to their communities of settlement. These relatives not only provided powerful cultural and economic incentives to move to these communities, but they also facilitated the process of migration by acting as host families.

Finally, as we might expect, relatives were especially important for more economically "vulnerable" members of New York society. Migrant women, migrant families with young children, and the migrant poor typically found both financial and emotional support from their relatives.

Among the thousands of migrating households of mid-nineteenth-century New York State, the Rosses, the Tetts, and the Levetts of rural Johnstown in Fulton County illustrate the crucial role of family connections for the ultimate survival of all. Thomas Ross, originally from England, was a landless laborer who had migrated to Johnstown in early 1855 with his pregnant wife, Elizabeth, her widowed mother, age fifty-three, and Elizabeth's younger brother, William Levett. The Rosses had followed Thomas' father, William Ross Sr., to New York and moved into a small frame house next door.[20]

But William Sr., age forty-eight, was not a successful man. He had settled in New York in 1848, and seven years later his occupation was listed as a "glove cutter" in a nearby factory. He and his family lived in a frame dwelling valued at less than one hundred dollars, and like his son, William Sr. owned no land. But despite his poverty, William Sr. managed to support his wife's aging parents, Robert and Grace Tett, both age sixty-three, as well as his own large family. In addition, it appears that he provided some support for his son Thomas and his family when they settled in Johnstown. These kin interrelations were common among New Yorkers at this time. Like many other families, the Tetts, the Rosses, and the Levetts found mutual support under challenging circumstances.

In short, relatives both inside and outside the household played a central role in the migration pageant of this changing society and underscore the importance of "chain migration" during this period. Migrants needed their families to help them survive this difficult process, and as we will see in Chapter 7, this need often was mutual.

LANDOWNERSHIP

Beyond the effect of one's age and family, landownership was an important factor in the migration of mid-nineteenth-century New Yorkers. In fact, of all the economic measures examined here, including occupation and home value, the ownership of land was the most important as a stabilizing force.

However, the causal relationship between landownership and migration is a bit ambiguous and difficult to interpret with these data. Did individuals move to a community with the intention of purchasing land and then remain? Or did people inherit land in a community and then decide to stay put? This research suggests that both scenarios were valid although further research is needed to clarify these relationships. What we can say with certainty, however, is that once New Yorkers either purchased or inherited land, they usually became more residentially stable and were less likely to move.

Seen another way, migration and tenancy often were associated. In fact, by mid-century, thousands of landless New Yorkers were being buffeted about the state in a seemingly endless series of short-range moves. William Wort and Ansel Cushman illustrate this residential instability. William, age forty-four, was listed as a landless farm laborer in 1855. He and his wife and seven children had migrated to Ellisburgh in Jefferson County in 1854, but before that, they had moved at least five times since the birth of their first child, William Jr. All nine family members lived in abject poverty, occupying a tiny log cabin that the census enumerator valued at only five dollars. Ansel Cushman, age forty-two, his wife, and their eight children also were recent in-migrants to rural Saratoga County in 1855. Their migration history paralleled that of the Wort family. In fact, both households represented one of the most transient groups in mid-nineteenth-century New York society: poor, landless farmers who often had many children. While the hope for a new beginning in a new community appeared to be one reason for their seemingly continual migration, for these two families at least, that new beginning quite often meant just one thing: more poverty and another move very soon.[21]

And yet, by middle age many poor New York farmers had been able to obtain a small farm, perhaps in a remote part of the state, and thereby break through the endless cycle of migration, tenancy, and poverty. George Ballard, age fifty-two, and Francis Foster, age forty-six, are good examples. Each of these men migrated with their families to Nanticoke Township in Broome County between 1845 and 1855, and an examination of their children's birthplaces reveals that both had moved about upstate New York most of their lives. However, by 1855 each had managed to obtain some farmland and participated occasionally in the market economy. In that year, both George and Francis produced more than one thousand pounds of butter, apples, and cider for market and a variety of grains for home consumption and sale. These two men had been transients in 1855, but by securing a bit of land, they apparently completed their migration by 1865 when both were still living in Nanticoke.[22]

In short, older men and women, native-born New Yorkers, those who had family connections in their communities, and landholders were less likely to have moved recently to communities in New York. On the other hand, younger New Yorkers, those born outside of the state, landless men and women, and those with few family ties were significantly more likely to have made a recent move. However, upstate urban and rural people were just as likely to have migrated during the middle years of the nineteenth century, and gender, ethnicity, marital status, and children in the household by themselves were not significantly related to continuous years of residence. Each of these groups had both stable and migratory members. Clearly, mid-nineteenth-century upstate New York was a mobile place with people from all walks of life participating in the pageant.

The "pastoral" nineteenth-century rural farmer
tending his calves.

CHAPTER 3

Pastoral Myths

I f migration was central to the personal transformation of thousands of rural Americans during the nineteenth century and instrumental to the agricultural transition in the middle of that century, then why have scholars generally ignored its role? This question is complex and fascinating, and its answer is firmly embedded in three enduring scholarly traditions. The first is the image of the migrant as the victim of modern industrial society; the second is the continuing search for the roots of American distinctiveness and the virtual enshrinement of the pioneer migrant; and the third is the pastoral myth that contrasts the dynamic, transient city with a static, immobile countryside. Each of these traditions has helped obscure our understanding of migration in nineteenth-century America.

THE MIGRANT AS VICTIM

One of the most powerful images of the migrant is that of a pathetic victim of economic change. The intellectual threads that have given substance to this image came initially from progressive historians and functionalist sociologists of the twentieth century. These scholars provided us with important insights into the problems that plagued American society, but in the process they promoted the stereotype of the migrant as a faceless casualty of the new economic order.

Progressive historians typically saw nineteenth-century American society in fundamental turmoil because of the forces of industrialization, capitalism, and urbanization. America's strength and uniqueness among the nations of the world seemed to be in jeopardy. Alas, we were becoming more "European," with all the problems of that "decadent" society. Vernon L. Parrington, for example, saw America's fall from primitive innocence beginning in the late eighteenth century with the emergence of the industrial economy and associated urban growth. He saw the spread of English liberalism as "concerned with exploitation ... rather than with justice and the rights of man." It "glorified the ... acquisitive instinct" and saw "social interests ... outside its legitimate sphere." For this scholar, the new order had little concern for common men and women, with capitalists colluding to "milk the cow and divide the milk among those who superintended the milking."[1]

Contemporaries of the progressives in the field of sociology also were influenced profoundly by the dramatic changes in society brought about by rapid industrialization and urbanization. They argued that these changes had destroyed the gemeinschaft of the traditional world, wrenched individuals from their primary social relationships, and plunged them into the sterile isolation of modern life. Georg Simmel, for example, felt that the individual had been reduced to a "negligible quantity ... a mere cog in an enormous organization of things and powers which tear from his hands all ... spirituality and value."[2]

The primary actor in this transition, of course, was the transient stranger, the migrant. This "fundamentally mobile person," Simmel noted, "[came] in contact at one time or another with every individual, but [was] not organically connected through established ties of locality and kinship with any single one."[3]

For Simmel, migrants were the first victims of urban industrial society, and their social life was characterized by an "atrophy of culture."[4] Similarly, Robert Park saw the migrant as the quintessential "marginal man" whose life was altered forever because of his physical and psychic distance from traditional (rural) society. He was the anonymous victim of urbanization and as a result, was both mentally and physically deficient.[5]

This view of migration seemed to be confirmed by related research in epidemiology. Writing in the mid-1930s, for example, Benjamin Malzberg argued that rates of mental illness among white migrants were more than three times higher than for the white population as a whole and nearly five times higher for black migrants than for blacks who did not move.[6] This tradition has continued. In the mid-1970s, Ronald Freedman studied more than 85,000 rural-urban migrants and noted that they were significantly more likely to have a disabling illness than those who had not moved.[7]

But while these scholars typically perceived the psychic trauma and physical maladies associated with moving as temporary, others suggested that there were long-term pernicious effects of migration on social organization and family life. Early on, for example, W.I. Thomas and Florien Znanecki had argued that the immigration experience of Polish peasants had led to the disintegration of their traditional folkways and mores.[8] Later, Ernest R. Mowrer and Pauline Young noted that the traditional Jewish family typically had been disrupted and sometimes destroyed as a result of immigration to the New World.[9] Historians also were influenced by these ideas. As noted in Chapter 2, Oscar Handlin borrowed heavily from them in his classic study of the "uprooting" aspect of immigration. He argued that the process of migration itself had been responsible for many of the problems experienced by nineteenth-century immigrants to America.[10]

As sociologist Harvey J. Locke explained it, migration was "the primary factor in family disorganization. ... [Moving] to a new location removes ... individuals or families from ... social restraints ... makes them free to violate traditional folkways and mores and allows them to express overtly behavior which had been inhibited because of social pressures. This makes it possible for divergent patterns to become more firmly entrenched."[11]

Earlier, Tocqueville had hinted that there was something insidious about the "restless nature" of Americans that had permanently altered if not destroyed the traditional family. In America, he said, "New families are constantly springing up, others are constantly falling away and all that remain change their condition. [This] makes every man forget his ancestors [and] hides his descendants ... from him."[12]

In short, migrants were not only mentally and physically deficient, but their families also were a mess! As a result, many saw the process of migration as a pathological one, the direct result of insidious changes in the "natural" order of human beings.

THE SEARCH FOR AMERICAN DISTINCTIVENESS

These scholars, who were often critical of rapid industrialization and unregulated capitalism, saw migrants, especially those moving to cities, as miserable victims of economic and social change. On the other hand, frontier historians searching for the roots of American distinctiveness (and greatness) saw migrants in a much more favorable light. Frederick Jackson Turner, for example, saw the essence of America's greatness in the fluidity and dynamism of the frontier, and he celebrated the experience of the migratory pioneer as being quintessentially American. The pioneer represented the driving force of American democracy and was the wellspring of the enduring ideal of rugged individualism. Turner argued that whereas those who remained behind in eastern cities and southern plantations might cling to the prejudices of their region, the nineteenth-century pioneer migrant had transcended sectionalism (the divisive force of that century) to create a new national cohesiveness and a vigorous democratic experiment. And while pioneers may have been suspicious of established government, they soon learned that only through cooperation could democracy and individualism coexist. In short, America's greatness derived from the migratory experiences of the pioneer.[13]

Over the years, some scholars have built on these general ideas. Most agreed that migration changed people, and more often than not they saw these changes as positive. Migration had forced Americans to become more pragmatic; it encouraged them to be more open and allowed them to adapt to the new problems and possibilities of nineteenth-century America.

George Pierson, a pioneer in the study of migration, noted that the very personal process of migration forced people to think differently about their lives and may have eroded those factors that inhibited individual change. He and others have argued that as migrants discarded many of their material possessions in preparation for a move, they were forced to consciously rank their belongings in terms of their utility and then decide whether or not to keep them. This often painful process helped foster a keen sense of pragmatism.[14]

But just as migrants discarded many of their material possessions, some jettisoned their "cultural baggage" as well. As Everett Lee has noted, migration may have encouraged individuals to abandon their traditional ideas and values. Lee argued that migrants seemed to have placed less importance on hereditary landownership because land could not be transported whereas money and skills could. As a result, he reasoned, the migrant's traditional relationship with the land may have been irrevocably changed.[15]

Thomas Cochran also noted this change among migrant American farmers who seemed to have had "no sentimental hereditary attachment to the particular plot of land that he initially acquired," perceiving it as a vehicle of upward mobility rather than the basis of social status.[16] In fact, for sociologists Alex Inkles and David Smith, these were some of the very characteristics of "modern" men and women who were open to new experiences, felt control over their environment, and then acted to produce change.[17] Finally, as H.G. Barnett has argued in his classic anthropological study of innovation, these were the essential traits of migrants, who were "characteristically receptive to new ideas whether they are developed by their own members or suggested by outsiders."[18]

For years, scholars have seen this openness to change and new experiences as a central feature of the migrant in American history. Although generally critical of migration, sociologist Georg Simmel admitted that the migrant was "freer, practically and theoretically; he surveys conditions with less prejudice; his criteria for them are more general and more objective ... he is not tied down in his action by habit or precedent."[19]

Similarly, Thomas Cochran argued that the early American migrant was a "risk taker" who often embraced new opportunities and challenges. In fact, for Cochran it was the continual migration of Americans that forced them to become innovative, creative, and open to new ideas and new ways of doing things. This encouraged Americans to become, in Cochran's words, "jacks of all trades but perhaps true masters of none." Continually faced with new challenges, the migrating American farmer was forced to innovate, experiment, and become flexible in order to solve the unique economic problems of a new environment.[20] This flexibility and innovation may have involved the application of traditional forms of production to new market realities or the adoption of a more scientific, businesslike approach to agriculture.

And more than a century ago Chevalier made a similar point, noting that "While the English[man] was very skillful ... he was lost when out of his special sphere." The American, on the other hand, had a "more general aptitude, his sphere is larger and he can extend it indefinitely at will."[21]

Finally, as Cochran has argued, migration not only affected the producer but the consumer as well. Americans who migrated were more willing to accept cheap, crudely manufactured American goods rather than demanding the precision and quality that would have been required of more expensive British or artisan products.[22] This nurtured a kind of culturally based "economic nationalism" that allowed American manufacturers to produce goods in large quantities using the available resources of the community and benefit from the principles of economies of scale.

For these scholars, then, migrants typically were open to change and new ideas, they were more pragmatic and innovative, and they saw land not just as a measure of social status but also as a means of upward social mobility. Moreover, their dramatic migration provided them with a portal through which they might enter the marketplace and emerging consumer culture.

Thus while the progressives saw urban migrants and immigrants as victims of industrial society, frontier historians and other scholars saw them as an embodiment of all that was good about America. These sharply contrasting archetypes have made it difficult for us to understand the process of migration in the past. It was as if Turner, the master interpreter of nineteenth-century America, had passed the intellectual baton to the progressive historian and functionalist sociologist who then evoked a very different interpretation of mobile American people. That swirling mass of humanity, characteristic of much of American history, was no longer seen as the engine of positive change but now was a kind of diaspora of helpless and rootless victims of urban industrial society. It is no wonder that we have had some difficulty understanding migration, considering its ambiguous position in American historiography.

THE PASTORAL MYTH

If the general process of migration has been obscured by enduring scholarly traditions, then our understanding of rural migration is even murkier. The persistent model of a transient, urban America and a static, pastoral countryside has been accepted historical dogma for generations. Moreover, problems in the measurement of migration in the past has reinforced that image and given it a veneer of scientific credibility.

For years, cities have been characterized as places of corruption, poverty, and crime inhabited by rootless, alienated transients. The contrasting rural, pastoral image, on the other hand, is embedded in the nineteenth-century republican notion of the stable, hardworking yeoman who provided the backbone of American society and democracy. For Jefferson it was very simple: "Those who labor in the earth are the chosen people of God ... while ... the mobs of great cities add just so much to the support of pure government as sores do to the strength of the human body. ... a degeneracy ... a canker which soon eats to the heart of its laws and constitution."[23]

As early as the eighteenth century, popular and intellectual perceptions of the migrant, especially the urban in-migrant, were almost universally negative. Writing in his *Poor Richard's Almanack,* for example, Benjamin Franklin once quipped "three removes is as bad as fire!"[24] And later in 1787 the *Pittsburgh Gazette* noted that Americans had an "unsettled disposition by inheritance."[25] By the 1850s even the superintendent of the U.S. Census lamented America's restlessness and blamed it on a "peculiar condition of this country."[26] Moreover, the metaphorical language used to describe urban migration typically reinforced this negative image. Migrants "flocked" to cities, "pouring" into new areas "in a steady stream," "flooding" labor markets and overwhelming city services.

Clearly, the "hordes" of migrants in American history presented a frightening image to what we now know was a relatively small, stable

American population. As Eric Monkkonen noted in his volume on tramping workers in the nineteenth century, vitriolic hostility toward migrants was quite common. One newspaper of the period approved of the goals of a group of locals "to fertilize their land with [migrants'] dead bodies ... as a ... permanent cure for the evil complained of." And later, the *Railroad Gazette* called upon the people to "exterminate these pests."[27]

Thus the long-standing popular tradition that sees urban development essentially as pathological and migrants as purveyors of social problems found a convenient counterpoint in a bucolic, peaceful, and immobile countryside. In recent years these popular images have been reinforced because of problems in the methodology of nominal record linkage, which have inflated significantly our quantitative estimates of urban population movement.

The current interest in the internal migration of nineteenth-century Americans began in the mid-1960s when Stephan Thernstrom documented the dramatic population turnover of laborers in Newberryport, Massachusetts.[28] Shortly thereafter, Peter Knights published his important study of migration to Boston at mid-nineteenth century, *The Plain People of Boston*.[29] Since then, historians have been fascinated by the social and physical development of American cities during the nineteenth century and the apparent rapid turnover of their populations. Indeed, as Michael Katz once noted, one of the two great themes of nineteenth-century urban history was population mobility.[30]

But was nineteenth-century urban America as transient as has been suggested by these and other studies? Clearly, the hypothesis of rapid population turnover in cities depends on the methodology of nominal record linkage, i.e., tracing individuals between two population lists.

In recent years historians have recognized a number of inherent imperfections in this technique as a method for measuring internal migration. The basic problem is that migration is measured as a residual: the difference in numbers between those who appear on a population list and those not found on the second. However, in addition to moving, people may be missing from the second source for at least three other reasons.

The first is death. Only recently have scholars of internal migration taken into account mortality occurring between two censuses. In the early 1980s, for example, Michael Katz, Michael Doucet, and Mark Stern estimated that 10.7 percent of the males and 9.9 percent of the females living in Buffalo, New York, in 1845 had died by 1855.[31] Similarly, Robert Barrows calculated that between 5 and 8 percent of the base population of Indianapolis, Indiana, in 1890 were dead ten years later.[32] But this sensitivity to demography in historical analysis is rare. Most studies of internal migration in the past have not estimated mortality during the decade, and as a result, decedents routinely have been counted as out-migrants. This omission has resulted in a consistent overstatement of internal migration (that is, it has understated persistence). This problem is especially acute in nineteenth-century cities where mortality was significantly higher than in rural areas. Thus, if death is counted as migration, cities typically will be seen as having a more migratory population.

People might also be missing from the second source because of enumerator omissions. Whether these enumerators were Census Marshalls or compilers of city directories, they made mistakes. Often they failed to count in the later enumeration some people who had been recorded in the former. An early hint as to the magnitude of this error came from the Philadelphia Social History Project.[33] When researchers attempted to link individuals from the Philadelphia census recount of November 1870 to the original census conducted five months earlier, they were able to find only 82.2 percent of those present on the recount document.[34] Although some people may have out-migrated during this five-month period, these figures suggest significant underenumeration. Similarly, by using Coale and Zelnik's figures, I estimated that a minimum of 4.4 percent of native-born white males in 1880 and 5.2 percent in 1890 were missed by the census taker. These figures were 3.4 and 4.9 percent, respectively, for women. And for young women aged thirty to thirty-four years, it was as high as 16.1 percent in 1890.[35] Finally, more recent research on census underenumeration during the nineteenth century from political science, economics, anthropology, and history suggests an underenumeration rate of about 15 percent for the population as a whole.[36]

Whatever the miss rate, the important point is that linkage error increases with underenumeration. And although it is difficult to determine how omissions in the census varied between communities, current research suggests that underenumeration was much more common in growing cities than in rural communities.[37] In urban areas, Census Marshalls may not have been as familiar with each household in a neighborhood. In less-populated rural areas, on the other hand, there was presumably more face-to-face contact, and thus underenumeration would probably have been less common. Once again, this problem tends to inflate significantly our estimates of population turnover in cities.[38]

Finally, many city dwellers were virtually "unlinkable" because of the "common name problem." Surnames of immigrants such as Smith, Johnson, and O'Brien were as common in cities in the past as they are today. No matter how hard the most dedicated and careful scholar might try to link these people, some will be counted as migrants even though they may have been living somewhere in the urban environs. Indeed, many of these so-called urban out-migrants may simply have made an intracity move and "disappeared" from the researcher's careful eye. Of course, the larger the city the greater the possibility for this kind of move and the greater the chance that the person might be missed by the researcher.[39]

Although many scholars have become aware of the existence of these difficulties, the evaluation of quantitative sources requires that we estimate the magnitude of the error involved in the record linkage study of mobility. Historians must turn to alternative sources and methods to assess the extent of mobility in nineteenth-century America and to measure differentials in mobility between urban and rural places during that century.

THE NEW YORK STATE CENSUS OF 1855

One document that allows us to measure directly the extent of internal migration in the past is the New York State Census of 1855. In that year, the state of New York, cognizant of the extent of its own population mobility, instructed enumerators to ask each individual in the household how long they had lived continuously in their communities.

Responses to this question allow us to compare levels of internal migration in rural and urban areas and determine statistically the degree to which nominal record linkage inflated our estimates of urban migration.[40]

This research (discussed in detail elsewhere) revealed first that the record-linkage process itself was responsible for a significant underestimation of population persister.ce in cities, i.e., a significant overstatement of urban population movement.[41] Also, the rate of population growth in a community was found to be a key factor in determining the success of the record-linkage process. This indicated that the technique of nominal record linkage was most *ineffective* in communities with especially high rates of growth, typically urban centers in nineteenth-century America.

In short, cities were often as stable (and sometimes more) as rural communities. This suggests that much of the internal migration during this period was from the countryside to the city or between rural communities and not just between or away from urban centers. Thus, the image of transient cities and stable rural communities stems in part from methodological problems of nominal record linkage and not entirely from actual population movement.

Of course, cities in the nineteenth century had many recent migrants in them, and as discussed in Chapter 2, a large proportion of these migrants were formerly from rural communities in this country and abroad. But many of these new arrivals did not out-migrate once they arrived. Despite the appearance of transiency in nineteenth-century cities, urban persistence rates were actually 7 percent *higher* on average than those in rural communities.[42]

A comparison of the population dynamics of rural Erie County with its bustling major city, Buffalo, illustrates these points and provides a more complete picture of population movement during this period. Buffalo was a classic boomtown during the middle of the century, nearly tripling its population from 24,777 to 74,217 in just ten years (1845–55). And although we might expect Buffalo to have been an extremely unstable community compared with rural Erie County, estimates of population movement tell a different story. In Buffalo, 71.4 percent of the 1855 residents arrived in that city between 1845 and

1855. But 77.1 percent of its original 1845 residents were still living there ten years later. In other words, only 22.9 percent of the original 1845 population had left Buffalo by 1855. People typically streamed into but not out of that city, a situation that contributed greatly to its rapid population growth during those years. In rural Erie County, on the other hand, people tended to circulate through the communities. While only 56 percent of the 1855 population of the county had arrived in the rural communities during the preceding decade, nearly half (49.6 percent) of its original 1845 population had left by 1855. Thus, whereas Buffalo resembled a population magnet, with people entering in large numbers and then staying, rural Erie County was more like a population revolving door, with a large proportion of its people moving in and out.[43]

Thus, by examining both in- and out-migration in these two areas, we get a very different picture of population mobility in the past. Indeed, Tocqueville may have been right after all. Much of the countryside was in constant motion during the nineteenth century, with thousands of farmers cultivating the land but leaving others to reap the harvest, to "go off elsewhere with their changing desires."[44]

An idealized vision of the traditional yeoman farm wife and her daughters in charge of dairy production.

The Traditional Yeoman

N ew York's culture of mobility was neither an isolated demographic phenomenon nor a "strange unrest" separate
from the dramatic social and economic changes occurring
in the middle of the nineteenth century. Rather, it was a pivotal
process at the center of these changes. But what was the nature of
these social and economic changes? The agricultural economy of New
York State during this period certainly witnessed a consistent movement toward the commercial marketplace. But how do we character-
ize the role of New York farmers in that shift? Did occasional involvement with the market constitute participation in the market
economy? Or was it necessary to produce a cash crop to be part of that
economy? In short, when did a farmer become "commercially oriented"? And when did a farm household become fully integrated into
that market economy? These questions are important, but their answers remain elusive.

This chapter will argue that market activity has been a part of the
American agricultural landscape for a long time. In fact, recent research has shown that a recognizable market economy had emerged in
New England around the middle of the eighteenth century. However,
most farmers at that time were not full participants in that economy. A
few regularly sold their produce on the open market and used the cash
from that sale to purchase artisan goods or an occasional import. But
our fascination with these farmers has obscured our understanding of
the vast majority of farming people who had occasional contact with

the market but clearly were part of a large, semi-subsistence yeoman class. Thus, although the market economy had emerged, the agricultural transition was not complete.

Slowly, this situation began to change. In the early nineteenth century, more farmers were drawn into the consumer culture, gradually embracing the ideas of scientific agriculture and a marketplace ethos. And by the middle of the century, most New York farmers were producing a marketable surplus. The emergence of the surplus market economy in the middle decades of the century completed the agricultural transition that began more than a century before.

THE NEW ENGLAND DEBATE REVISITED

For over twenty-five years, colonial historians have debated vigorously the timing and emergence of the marketplace in North America. This literature is lively and sometimes overwhelming. It is built on imaginative political and theoretical interpretations as well as a growing body of empirical data. However, despite this interesting literature, the debate remains polemical and tends to obscure our understanding of agricultural change. There are at least two problems here. The first is the difficulty in interpreting the goals of farmers in the past, and the second centers on the definition of market involvement. The underlying question seems to be whether farmers of the colonial period (and early nineteenth century) saw agriculture primarily as a business or simply as a way of life. Or was it a mixture of both?

One of the earliest historical images of farmers in the eighteenth and early nineteenth century was what Richard Hofstadter has called the "happy yeoman." This image of early farmers as sturdy, self-sufficient, hardworking, egalitarian souls who sought an independent existence and shunned market dependence and financial debt is rooted deeply in American iconography. These farmers were the backbone of the American democratic society and economy.[1]

Hofstadter, of course, argued that this image was overly simplistic and romantic. But while he debunked the happy yeoman, he replaced it with yet another stereotype of latent businessmen farmers whose entrepreneurial instincts were held in check only by the lack of market opportunities. For Hofstadter, "[the] farmer in most cases was in fact inspired to make money ... and ... self sufficiency was usually forced upon him by a lack of transportation or markets, or by the necessity to save cash to expand his operations."[2]

This historiographical perspective flourished throughout the 1950s as American agriculture seemed to have reached the pinnacle of its success. By the mid-1960s James T. Lemon provided what many felt was conclusive empirical evidence of a widespread commitment to the marketplace by the eighteenth century. Lemon argued that by 1750, 80 percent of all southeastern Pennsylvania farmers were selling a surplus on the open market.[3] Although these estimates were challenged, many scholars interpreted them as evidence of early and widespread commercialization.

Douglass North also saw early commercial agricultural activity, although he dated it to the early nineteenth century. He argued that by the 1830s a pattern of interregional trade, what he referred to as the counterclockwise trade pattern, had already developed in the United States. This pattern suggested extensive commercial agriculture and regional specialization by that date.[4] Despite the fact that Albert Fishlow and others demonstrated that North's estimates were exaggerated, the notion of an early and widespread commitment to the market economy continued.[5]

Most agricultural historians recognized the existence of many semi-subsistence yeoman farmers throughout this period. But even the most discerning among them, such as Percy Bidwell and John Falconer, assumed that they existed only because of a lack of an effective transportation infrastructure and urban markets. For these scholars the "outstanding characteristic of the farm economy of the early settlements [was] ... production for consumption and not for sale. ... [But] as distant markets became accessible by improved transportation facilities ... [and] with an outlet for their produce thus provided, farmers were stimulated to increase production."[6] In short, nineteenth-century farmers, like their city cousins, were businessman with well-developed entrepreneurial instincts.

Despite this prevailing historiography, some historians were troubled by claims of early and widespread commercialization of the agricultural economy. But this argument was not effectively challenged until James Henretta published his study of the attitudes and values of preindustrial American farmers. Henretta articulated what many historians had felt all along: that nonmarket agriculture and the traditional values associated with it had persisted well into the nineteenth century even in the face of growing market opportunities.[7]

In recent years, a number of historians from the "new rural history" have built on this basic premise. Christopher Clark, Michael Merrill, Robert Mutch, Thomas Dublin, and others have argued that American farmers of the late eighteenth and nineteenth centuries were not always "latent capitalists." These scholars contend that the agricultural economy of these years was a "strange brew" of both semi-subsistence and commercial activities.[8]

To understand the transition to the cash economy, for example, Christopher Clark has argued that we must first understand fully both kin relationships and production patterns of households in the past. For Clark, kinship structured the emerging commercial economy and slowed the process of individualism associated with the commercial profit-seeking motive.[9]

Similarly, Michael Merrill has ignored the subsistence-surplus dichotomy and instead has focused on the nature of exchange within the "household mode of production." For Merrill, this mode of production was based on a set of exchanges of labor and not commodities, and therefore surpluses were both irrelevant and detrimental to the continued existence of that economy.[10]

In the last decade, this debate has taken a slightly different direction. Bettye Hobbs Pruitt has demonstrated that market involvement did not necessarily mean profit orientation. In her analysis of a sample of late-eighteenth-century Massachusetts household probate inventories, she found that "many farms, especially poorer ones, could not have been self-sufficient in food." As a result, these farmers often "entered into exchange not for profit ... but simply to feed their families."[11]

Winifred Barr Rothenberg expanded this general argument. In her critique of what she calls the "moral economy model" of New England during this period, she noted that the market economy predated the "technological capacity or resource abundance to produce surpluses." For Rothenberg, the market economy, as measured by the "convergence of farm account book prices and wages," probably emerged in New England in the mid-eighteenth century.[12] Clearly, occasional market involvement was common in the late eighteenth and nineteenth centuries.

While these new interpretations have not settled the New England debate, they have helped us appreciate the complexities and individual variations in the first phase of the agricultural transition. And perhaps more importantly they have given us some insights into the role of the family and the household in the movement to the market economy.

Certainly we can now agree that participation in the market economy has been a part of the American landscape for some time, perhaps even before Rothenberg's mid-eighteenth-century estimate. When transportation costs decline and legal institutions that protect contracts and property rights are established, market participation, however tentative, will begin with the poor trading for basic subsistence and the rich selling their surplus crop for cash. Pruitt demonstrated that very poor late-eighteenth-century farmers sold part of their crop simply to survive. Similarly, Alan Taylor has shown that poor farmers on the Maine frontier typically exploited the rich game and timber resources of their community and sold these products for cash rather than clearing additional farmland for their own subsistence. Finally, semi-subsistence farmers at mid-nineteenth century like Porter Bliss of New York spent a great deal of time involved in agricultural "sustaining industries" such as cutting timber, manufacturing stave bolts, and stripping hemlock bark for market. Porter typically balanced these activities with the production of primary agricultural products.[13]

In short, as Alan Taylor has noted recently, the New England debate over the timing and emergence of the market economy tends to "obscure the economic dualities of rural life." For a variety of reasons, most farming people of this period had contact with the market.[14]

But another central question remains: What was the extent of individual farm production during this period? Certainly there was a difference between a poor dirt farmer, living in poverty, who sold (or exchanged) staves, hemlock bark, or maple syrup to supplement his subsistence and a successful surplus market farmer producing a cash crop and from its sale purchasing a wide variety of consumer goods. Each of these farmers was a part of a growing market economy, but their level of involvement in that economy differed substantially.

Thus, by understanding differences in agricultural production, we can begin to see the completion of the agricultural transition at mid-nineteenth century. By then, most farmers in New York State had begun to produce a marketable surplus. This transition was important because it signaled the birth of modern agriculture as well as the rapid consolidation of the agricultural economy.

ESTIMATING NET PRODUCTION

At the heart of any estimate of the net production of mid-nineteenth-century farmers is the question of how much food they consumed. If we assume that they ate very little, then our estimates of agricultural production will be greater. On the other hand, if we assume that daily caloric consumption was high, then our net production estimates will be considerable lower. Thus, the question of food consumption is central to our understanding of agricultural production.

In his pioneering work on this question in the 1960s, James T. Lemon examined widows' pensions among late-eighteenth-century Pennsylvania farmers in Lancaster and Chester counties. Lemon assumed that "widows' [annual food] requirements were about average for a family of five or six"[15] and consisted of 150 pounds of meat, the dairy production of two cows, ten to fifteen bushels of grain, as well as fruit, fleeces, and a horse.[16] Lemon then estimated that this annual production would require seventy-three to seventy-eight acres of land.[17] Since the "median values of the average sizes of farms ... was about 125 acres,"[18] then "the average farm sold at least 40 percent of its production."[19]

But Lemon's daily caloric allowances were too low. His figures show that this frugal diet amounted to less than 1500 calories per day, with a daily allotment of only 1.3 ounces of meat! This is considerably lower than the diets reported for American slaves, prisoners, and children in the Norwich Hospital in 1632 and is less than one-half the meager rations of the Continental Army in 1780.[20]

Moreover, in recent years a number of scholars have estimated that even the daily caloric consumption of eighteenth- and nineteenth-century urban poor and working-class people in Europe was significantly higher than Lemon's figures. Carole Shammas, for example, estimated daily caloric consumption in eighteenth-century English workhouses of between 2000 and 2500; Robert Fogel set the figure at about 2700 for late-eighteenth-century England as a whole; Cormac Ó. Gráda estimated it at 3100 for nineteenth-century Ireland; and John Komlos figured 2700 calories per day for eighteenth-century workers in Austria. Finally, Geert Bekaert has shown that the median caloric consumption of adult males in nineteenth-century Belgium was about 2500 calories per day. This meant that about 20 percent of Belguim's urban population lacked sufficient physical energy "to enter the workforce on a permanent basis."[21]

But although Lemon's estimates of caloric consumption appear to be too low, many scholars have built on his work without much criticism of his assumptions. As a result, they probably have overstated early American farmers' surplus production.[22]

Some agricultural historians and economists, on the other hand, have used a much more generous daily caloric allowance. Geert Bekaert estimated that an "average" man (172 centimeters tall) doing "moderate work" required 4169 calories per day, whereas a large man (180 centimeters) toiling eight hours each day needed 5750 calories per day. Similarly, the World Health Organization estimates a diet of 4000 calories as sufficient for moderate activity. Finally, Atack and Bateman and McInnis have estimated a slightly higher daily caloric equivalent of 5200 for this period. These estimates were derived from extant diet records and confirm literary evidence as well as contemporary accounts of food consumption that suggest that ordinary Americans in the eighteenth and nineteenth centuries consumed an extraordinary amount of food.[23]

In his travels around Poughkeepsie in 1842, for example, William Thompson noted that for workingmen the morning snack consisted of "some kind of meat—sometimes fowls, hot breads, raw onions with vinegar and pepper, mush, pickles [and] buckwheat cakes—smoking hot which were very good when buttered on both sides and eaten with molasses."[24] Similarly, James Stuart, writing of his travels in New York State in the late 1820s, noted that meals were "liberal in point of quantity." He also pointed out that Americans "seem universally to eat more animal food than the British ... and to eat quickly." His two-course dinner consisted of "large lobsters and fowls [with] roasted and broiled potatoes and vegetables of various kinds." And if that were not enough, for dessert there were "pies, puddings and cheese."[25] Even for tea, Americans seemed to eat a great deal. On his tour of New York and the Erie Canal, John Howison wrote of tea time in the village of Auburn in upstate New York. He noted that the simple fare "was abundantly furnished with beef-steaks, ham, fowls, preserved fruit cake, cheese, etc."[26] And to top off the day, Edward Coke wrote, somewhat disapprovingly, of one midnight snack he had in the autumn of 1832 that consisted of "apple pie, new cheese, ... beer, heavy Indian bread and port wine." Then off to bed because very soon breakfast would be served! Although not all Americans ate in such quantities, it would appear that those with access to food (such as farmers) probably consumed a great deal, certainly much more than most of us do today.[27]

It also seems likely that nineteenth-century farmers would have required greater caloric intake because they expended a great deal of energy in their daily work: chopping wood, plowing fields, cutting and bailing hay, cradling oats, washing clothes, and cleaning. Moreover, there must have been substantial waste and spoilage during this period before refrigeration, a fact that must affect our calculations of food consumed. For all of these reasons, any estimate of the caloric consumption of nineteenth-century American farmers must be generous.

This analysis follows the lead of Atack and Bateman and McInnis and uses a daily consumption figure of 5200 calories for an adult male. Once consumption was determined, estimates of net surplus production at the farm level were possible (see Appendix 2). The general formula used was $S = T - G - F - H$, where S is surplus production expressed in bushels of corn equivalents, T is total farm production expressed in bushels of corn equivalents, G is seed requirements for the next year, F is feed requirements for the current year, and H is human consumption.

Briefly, all agricultural yields listed in the 1855 and 1865 New York State Agricultural Census manuscripts were converted into a common caloric metric: bushels of corn equivalents. The decision to convert to calories rather than prices was made to avoid reliance on the rather maddening price fluctuations of this period. However, in the case of nonfood products such as silk, wool, and cloth, "opportunity costs" were estimated. Once these conversions were made, net yield estimates were calculated for each farm in the sample for 1855 and 1865. These figures allow us to examine net yield differentials between individual farm families at different stages of the life cycle in different market areas and over time.

THE NATURE OF AGRICULTURE AT MID-CENTURY

What was the extent of surplus market involvement at mid-nineteenth century? In 1855 just over half (55.2 percent) of the sampled farmers produced a surplus for market, whereas 44.8 percent did not produce enough food (or its equivalent) to feed their own families. Thus, it would appear that many of these farmers participated in the marketplace on an occasional basis, perhaps just to provide their families with food they did not produce.

But to understand fully the various strategies these farmers used to achieve self-sufficiency in food (and then perhaps to produce a marketable surplus), we must consult sources such as diaries, the popular literature of the period, the agricultural press, and newspapers. An examination of these materials demonstrates that in order to supplement their meager yields, many of these farmers maintained older forms of household production, fished and hunted regularly, and often were involved in a number of traditional "sustaining industries," such as the production of potash, cordwood, charcoal, hemlock bark, or barrel staves.

Also, many of these farm men and women engaged in a complex network of labor exchange. This might include the barter of two hours of pulling tree stumps or stripping hemlock bark for a predetermined amount of flour, grain, or fresh produce. Interestingly, these traditional forms of production were not limited to the yeoman class. Many nineteenth-century surplus market farmers maintained "traditional" forms of production that were labor intensive and communal in nature. And ironically, these "traditional" forms of production helped some farmers produce a surplus during this decade.

WOMEN AND AGRICULTURAL PRODUCTION

The bridge between yeomanry and surplus market production was a difficult one to cross, and women often played a facilitating role. Earlier in the century a farm woman might have produced some wool or flax cloth for barter or sold piecework to an itinerant merchant. But as factory-made cotton textiles became more available after the 1830s, New York farm women, looking for additional sources of barter or cash, adapted to new economic realities. While a few may have labored in textile factories for a time to supplement the family's income, most continued to work in the home and maintained traditional familial relationships.

Thomas Dublin's study of "outwork" among New Englanders illustrates how women in one village tentatively entered the cash economy within the traditional household culture. Farm wives and daughters often found time in their busy schedules to construct palm hats for Dexter Whittemore's country store. They then used credits from this production to barter for agricultural goods, textiles, "store-bought" clothing, "third-party payments," and later on, cash. In fact, between 1830 and 1850, the proportion of all transactions involving cash increased from about 43 percent to more than 62 percent, and barter declined significantly. Clearly, these women had entered the market economy while maintaining their traditional position within the household, attending to the duties of wife, mother, or daughter.[28]

This relationship to the market economy was common during the nineteenth century. Women in upstate New York often dried fruit, knitted stockings and mittens, or made quilts to sell or barter to the local merchant. William G. Holbrook, a mid-nineteenth-century itinerant peddler from upstate New York, has provided us with a number of examples of this type of economy. During these years Holbrook recorded in his diary that he typically purchased "the barter of both farmer and wife." In late August of 1854, for example, he arose at six in the morning and "drove to a local village, took breakfast ... and afterwards purchased of A. Knight and E. Martin their farmers' barter." Later he traveled to the small town of Jeffersonville where he "received socks" from a farmer's wife. In that same month he "bot some barter from [a farm family that included] copper, brass and hair." Apparently, all products, both agricultural and tonsorial, were part of the rural exchange economy.[29]

Other farm women found sources of income in the production of potash or pearl ash, which had become important industrial commodities in the nineteenth century. Potash and its finer cousin, pearl ash, were the primary components of alum, a material essential in the production of paper. Similarly, they were the principal source of saltpeter used in the commercial preservation of meat and the manufacture of gunpowder and soap as well as a cotton cloth bleach in the production of textiles.[30]

Before the 1830s wood ash was a typical product of the semi-subsistence yeoman farm. A pioneer farmer would girdle a stand of hardwood and later would set fire to the trees for easier removal. The ashes then would be collected, processed, and either sold or bartered. In this way, the yeoman farmer could supplement his subsistence or household income for the first year or two on the homestead and thus could afford the basic necessities of hardscrabble farm life. But with the introduction of the crosscut saw and the growing demand for cordwood, the girdling method of tree removal became both unnecessary and unprofitable. It simply made better economic sense to cut the timber for cordwood or lumber or convert it to charcoal.

But women still produced wood ashes (sometimes called house ashes) from cooking and other household activities. Crude potassium carbonate could be made by boiling in large pots the lye made from these ashes and then allowing the mixture to evaporate. This kind of work could be integrated into the daily schedules of most women. And until the late 1850s, when large deposits of potassium were discovered

in places such as Strassburg, Germany, most of this product was produced by women on semi-subsistence farms.[31]

Women could earn extra cash by selling ashes to country merchants because during these years the price of wood ash more than doubled from about ten to twenty-two cents per bushel. Similarly, as mentioned above, potash and pearl ash were an important medium of
exchange in the rural barter economy. Dorothy Brady has shown that in
1839 one pound of pearl ash could be exchanged for about 9 buttons,
30 hooks and eyes, 90 pins, or 4 matches. By 1860 the same amount of
pearl ash could be traded for 15 buttons, 51 hooks and eyes, 156 pins,
or 13 matches. This "allowed women to acquire clothing and gee gaws
that began to appear in country stores in the 1840s."[32]

In addition to these products, the time-honored tradition of women
milking the cow to provide cream and butter for the farm table continued throughout this period. By mid-nineteenth century, however, dairy
products had become important market commodities. New York farmers had begun to realize that they could no longer compete with midwestern farmers in the production of field crops, especially grains. But
dairying was a different story. Here, proximity to market was still a critical factor, and as a result, milk, cheese, and especially butter became
important market products that could provide a family with some extra
cash or barter. Moreover, dairying also could satisfy those who desired
a profit but were unwilling to abandon traditional methods of farmwork. While the investment in some new tools and agricultural machines may have been too expensive or perhaps culturally unaccept-
able, dairy production could be increased simply by adding a few hands
to the production process. Once again, by mid-century, what traditionally was "women's work" had become commercial production that
could make a critical difference to yeomen farm families in search of a
small agricultural surplus.

The sale of potash, butter, knitting, dried fruit, or even hair allowed women to enter the market economy and gave them a chance to
purchase or barter for things that were available from the itinerant peddler or merchant at the country store. Moreover, her work often provided a critical link to the surplus market economy for the entire farm
household. For these women, little had changed. After all, supplement-

ing the subsistence of the farm family with a bit of barter was an old and honored tradition. The difference now was the growth of the market economy in more remote rural areas and the availability of diverse consumer commodities designed especially for her and her family. Like many of their more materialistic menfolk who seemed continually to ponder the purchase of a new buggy, wagon, plow, or a new farm in the next county, women also were being drawn into the seductive web of consumerism and materialism.

And yet while women often played an important role in the transition from semi-subsistence yeomanry to surplus market production, their economic role in production began to change as their families became more integrated into the market economy. As cash transactions gradually came to dominate both barter and labor exchange, some farm households assumed the ideals of the new farmer: scientific production and specialization of labor based on gender. According to this developing creed, men were to attend to the commercial activities and production on the farms while women were to assume the role of the mistress of the orderly home and provide a haven from the increasingly complex business world in which the men were engaged. These ideas will be developed more fully in the next chapter, but the irony is worth noting here that the more a woman contributed to changing economic patterns, the less she was expected to be an active part in the new economy.

FOREST PRODUCTS

While the production of potash or dairy products for market was usually the work of women on the semi-subsistence yeoman homestead at mid-nineteenth century, men often used the forest to produce a variety of products to supplement their agricultural production. Throughout this period, wood remained the basic source of fuel for heating and material for homes, fences, utensils and, until the 1840s, most agricultural implements. So an enterprising yeoman farmer might work, for instance, as a part-time cooper during the off-season. Wooden barrels were always needed for the packaging of most commodities such as flour, meat, cider, vinegar, fish, and fruit. And if his skills were not well enough developed as a "tight cooper" (that is, he could not produce a

water-tight barrel), he might work as a "slack cooper" or simply produce staves for the barrels themselves. It was said that an industrious
farmer (presumably with the help of a grown son or relative) could produce a thousand staves per year and supplement the subsistence of the
household quite nicely.[33]

Porter Bliss, the New York farmer mentioned above, often
recorded this kind of activity in his diary. On August 2, 1854, for example, after a morning hay harvest, he wrote that he and Dan "went to
draw some stave bolts out of the woods." A few days later, the two
"drew a load of stave bolts" and the next morning "went to [Caskeys]
with my bolts [and] received $5.25." With this cash Porter "paid Mrs.
Stone for a sack of flour that I got for Dan," who in return "helped father with the mowing."[34]

The rest of Porter's month was filled with traditional field work,
but increasingly he mentioned the "manufacture" of staves. On August
25 he "went up to Caskeys with a load of stave bolts," and on September 3, "Dan helped saw bolts." The next day, Porter "went up to
Spenser's after a waggon [and] helped Munson get out a load of bolts
and draw a load for myself." The following day, the crew returned to
"Caskey's with a load of bolts," and for the next month this labor continued without much interruption. One "load of bolts" was drawn on
September 6 and four more on September 8. Then on September 10,
"father and Munson drew up each a load of bolts ... enough to come to
$14.50." When Porter sprained a knee on September 15, his labor was
slowed a bit. Nevertheless, he recorded in his diary that the crew continued their production of staves at least five more times in the month
that followed.[35]

In dairying regions of the state, firkins also were in great demand.
A firkin was a wooden container carved from the trunk of a tree. It held
about 112 pounds of butter and was a standard market container
throughout the century. In addition to the production of milk, cheese,
and butter, it was estimated that a farmer could make about three firkins
per day, each selling for about a dollar. Moreover, if he was skillful
with an axe, a wide array of other wooden containers, such as soap
buckets, water pails, and churns, also found ready markets in both the
barter and emerging cash economies.[36]

In areas where large stands of oak or hemlock were still available, numerous other opportunities existed. The bark of these trees was essential in tanning leather, and throughout this period tanning remained a decentralized industry supplementing the incomes of thousands of farm families. For these reasons most farmers of this period recognized the potential source of income from hemlock bark.

Rice Cook, an itinerant surveyor, kept a diary and recorded brief descriptions of the most impressive features of the lands he had surveyed for sale. Cook typically mentioned the availability of hemlock bark. In Broome County, for example, he wrote of a plot of "land, valuable for culture and hemlock timber."[37] And in that same year he noted a farm in Cattaraugus County with poor land but which had "some good trees of hemlock."[38] Moreover, most farm journals of the period regularly mentioned the availability of hemlock on farms as a lure to potential buyers.[39]

But although hemlock bark offered potential profit for the strong farmer with equally strong sons or relatives in the household, stripping it was strenuous work. Porter Bliss' diary from the summer of 1854 suggests the sheer drudgery of this labor in the hot, mosquito-infested forests of New York. From July 16 through the end of August when Porter returned to more conventional agricultural pursuits, he and his friends Asher and Munson as well as his father "worked at the bark." Porter took one day off on July 21 and "staid home and watched the bees," but he returned to the hemlock forest the next day. One gets the sense that he was overjoyed when on August 1 "it rained so that we had to quit" (early). Nevertheless, he soon returned to the forest for three solid weeks of peeling bark until August 21. Following that intensive labor, Porter and his father began the harvest. On August 22, exhausted, Porter's entry was simply: "cradled oats."[40]

If the farm family had access to a river, canal, or other waterway, there was always the possibility of cutting timber for market. Cordwood, of course, was the primary domestic fuel at this time, and its industrial use had grown dramatically. In fact, throughout the nineteenth century, New Yorkers were the largest producers of cordwood in the United States. The greater Salina Saltworks, for example, produced more than three million bushels of salt annually by the 1840s and used more than 200,000 cords of wood in their furnaces each year. Similarly, it has been estimated that the New York Central railroad used about 360,000 cords annually. It seemed that the demand for this product was insatiable.[41]

A "good man," the farm journals tell us, could cut a cord of wood in a day, and if he were able to sustain this labor (which is very doubtful for most men), he could clear an acre in an off-season. This amounted to about sixty cords of wood or more. In fact, through his reading of farmers' diaries from Lewis, Montgomery, and Seneca counties during this period, Paul Gates has estimated that it was not unusual for farmers to spend from five to eight weeks (thirty-nine to fifty-four days) just cutting, preparing, and transporting cordwood to market. This represented a substantial commitment (about 15 percent of their total work days) for these farmers and underscores, once again, the importance of this product. Of course, the farm family first had to meet their own fuel needs (perhaps as much as ten to twelve cords per year) before they could consider producing some for market. Nevertheless, for an aggressive, hard-working, strong, commercially oriented farmer and his equally strong male relatives, there was potential profit in the dark forests of New York State.[42]

Porter Bliss was one such farmer. For Porter, the off-season began immediately after the harvest and lasted well into the long New York winter. His work schedule for the month of December 1854, for example, reveals that from December 12 through December 20, he and his father labored in the woods to finish the season's timber work, presumably for both cordwood and lumber. Then, after a short break, during which an unusually large amount of snow fell (this was western New York after all), they returned to work on Christmas Day and continued straight through to New Year's Eve working "at the timber." Perhaps as a kind of symbolic gesture, the two celebrated the New Year by pushing "twenty-three logs off" down the river to the saw mill several miles away. The year's work had come to an end, but, as his diary informs us, it would begin again very shortly.[43]

More skill was required but greater profits could be earned in the production of charcoal, the primary fuel of the nineteenth-century blacksmith, tinsmith, and metalworker. Charcoal also was an essential ingredient in gunpowder and was prized as a polisher and deodorizer.

A farmer and, say, two grown sons or relatives could earn substantial profits from several months of intense labor in the frigid winter woods of upstate New York.

But the production of charcoal was no easy task. Hardwoods such as elm produced the best charcoal. The enormous trees were felled and then cut into three- to five-foot lengths. These were placed lengthwise, like spokes of a wheel, around a kindling fire. More logs were added to the original pile until as many as thirty to forty cords of wood were in place. This labor represented a great deal of work for three grown men and perhaps several boys working as helpers. The log pile, sometimes twenty to thirty feet in diameter or more, was ignited and then covered with earth and sod with a few air holes to allow the fire to get started. When it was going well, the air holes were covered with mud and the fire was thus controlled. For at least ten days and as long as three to four weeks, the "burner" would carefully tend the pyre, constantly guarding against an outbreak of fire and then covering it quickly with more mud or dirt. A raging inferno could easily destroy everything. One cord of wood could yield as much as thirty bushels of charcoal, with some operations producing one thousand to twelve hundred bushels of charcoal. This could amount to more than two hundred dollars for an off-season of labor.[44]

While a farmer, several adult workers, and a couple of helpers could produce substantial profits from the production of charcoal, stave bolts, or hemlock bark, not all farm families enjoyed this kind of human capital. In fact, unless a farm family could recruit relatives from other communities to work for board, there were precious few years during the life course of any farm family that this level of labor could be sustained. If sons were too young, fathers were too old, one of the key workers was injured, or a family member was sick, this kind of intense labor would be impossible to complete. In Chapter 7 we will explore the ramifications of this argument. At this point it is sufficient to note that many successful, surplus-oriented farm households during this period supplemented their labor by recruiting migrating kin (and other boarders) into their households where an exchange of room and board for labor often was made to the benefit of both migrant and host family.

But even if the family did not have this kind of human capital, the forests of New York still offered opportunities for supplemental income or barter. One of these was the production of maple syrup, which traditionally was harvested and produced as a communal family enterprise. The maple syrup harvest usually began in April when weather conditions allowed the sap to run. It then was collected by men and young boys and boiled in large pots by the women of the household. A farm family could tap and produce maple syrup from as many as five hundred large trees (about six to eight acres) in a season, and in a good year each tree could yield about fifty cents worth of syrup. Thus a farm household potentially could earn two hundred dollars or more in a spring harvest, although few realized this kind of profit.

For Delos Hackley of Batavia, New York, the maple syrup season of 1862 began on Saturday, March 22, when he "drew the buckets to the woods." The following Wednesday, he "drew some wood to the boiling place [and] tapped 130 trees." The family then "boiled sap" on Friday and Monday, March 28 and 31, and gathered "four pails of syrup" on April 1. The next day they repeated the process, "drew wood to the boiling place and gathered sap," and on April 3 they "syruped down, had 8 pails of syrup." Finally, beginning on April 7, the family "gathered sap ... boiled sap and syruped down" at least five more times until April 16 when Delos "commenced to plow for peas."[45]

The maple sap was boiled until it "sugared," making a kind of granulated sugar or "patty pancake" as it was called at the time. If the process was stopped before sugaring began, however, a thick maple syrup or molasses was produced. Each of these products could be marketed. But the initial capital outlay for buckets, spiles, covers, and vats could be expensive, and as a result most farm families had to resort to more primitive, though less efficient, homemade equipment. Moreover, the international sugar cane monopolies often glutted the market with this sweetener, depressing the price of syrup and making it a bitter product indeed.[46]

Nevertheless, the production of maple syrup and other by-products of the forest and farm, such as apples, honey, and beeswax, was extremely popular throughout this period. Like dairying, each of these products was ideally suited to those farm households that wanted to produce for market but were unwilling to alter significantly their traditional forms of production.

Some farmers saw these products simply as a supplement to their diet or as a product to barter, whereas others were able to use them to generate a cash surplus for their family. John Hull, for example, was able to produce a surplus during this decade (1855–65), primarily through increased production of field crops, dairying, and wool production. But this hard-working farmer and his family of five (including two boarding relatives) also produced a number of products from the available resources of the homestead. These included fifty bushels of apples, two barrels of cider, one hundred pounds of honey, five pounds of beeswax, six pounds of maple syrup, and five gallons of maple molasses.[47]

Others, like Abjah Ransom of Washington County, produced eight hundred pounds of maple syrup for market and as a result was able to make the transition from yeoman to surplus market producer. In fact, Ransom and his family entered the market economy despite the fact that their production of both dairy products and field crops actually declined during this decade.[48]

In short, the forest offered products to the industrious, market-oriented farm family as well as the yeoman household producer. Moreover, these products were available with modest cash outlays but rather large "investments" in human capital as well as household cooperation.

TRADITIONAL LABOR EXCHANGES

Once again, it is important to remember that not all farmers worked to produce a surplus. Many exchanged their labor for agricultural commodities or land, traded their labor for the labor of others, or simply used these products for barter. One account of these kinds of transactions comes from a diary of Porter Bliss, who by the end of the Civil War had become a successful surplus market farmer. On May 28, 1865, he recorded a labor exchange with his neighbor, Asher: "Asher came down this morning and looked over accounts with us. He is owing me $7.72 in deal for which he turns over to me logs on the bank at $1 per log."[49]

Other entries demonstrate that Porter also found time to help his neighbors. This investment of energy and goodwill would be repaid later when he too would need the help of the community. His entry of

June 4, 1865, for example, shows that he and Munson went "up to John Berlers to a plantin bee"[50] and later to Mrs. Smith's (the widow) for a "raising."[51]

Porter's diary also indicates that there often was a fluid exchange of labor between farmers that ignored typical status distinctions. This kind of "traditional" labor exchange was typical of many mid-nineteenth-century farmers. Porter's father, for example, was a successful commercial farmer and had a strong team of oxen that he often used to help both neighbors and hired hands. On June 5, he "went over to Munsons with the oxen and plowed." Then in partial return for this work "Munson plowed a little for me." This three-way exchange of labor was commonplace. Munson owned neither an ox nor a horse, but he did have a colt that Porter wrote he bartered "to father for two acres of land adjoining mine."[52] In return for the plowing, Munson worked for Porter that same day and on June 11 and 12 helped Porter and Asher "raft logs ... down to the mill."[53]

Thus while there were no cash transactions between Munson and the Bliss family, the barter of the colt for the land and labor for plowing benefited each farm household. This exchange of labor was commonplace, but only through an examination of informal evidence such as diaries can we appreciate both its extent and importance. Clearly, this kind of economy was seldom recorded in formal account books and certainly cannot be calculated from the agricultural schedules of the census.

Finally, other farmers supplemented their agricultural production with a secondary occupation. As Tocqueville noted just a few years before, "Almost all farmers of the United States combine some trade with agriculture."[54] Twenty-five-year-old Henry Dutchess, for example, was employed as a laborer and supported his twenty-two-year-old wife Clarissa and their two children. But he also rented an acre of land to help supplement the family's income. Henry did not plow the land in 1855 but kept it in pasture, presumably for the two cows from which the family (probably Clarissa) produced 100 pounds of butter as well as some milk for the table. Clarissa also raised chickens, eggs, and one pig for market.[55] In that same village, Samuel Pitcher, a shoemaker, raised a cow that produced 125 pounds of butter for market, and George Robinson, a carpenter, sold 125 pounds of butter. Although meager, this

kind of production provided these households with some cash to purchase a few extras from the country store or perhaps a bit of food to
supplement their subsistence.[56]

Each of these three farm families owned or rented land, each had
tenuous ties to the market economy, and each household head retained
a secondary occupation ranging from unskilled to skilled work. Each,
it should be noted, apparently out-migrated from their village sometime
after 1855.

While Henry Dutchess, Samuel Pitcher, and George Robinson appear to have been nonagricultural workers first and involved only marginally with the market economy, Robert Teneyck clearly was a farmer
first and a carpenter second. Robert, thirty-nine, plowed twenty acres of
land in 1855 (a substantial amount), but his field crop harvest was
abysmal, yielding only ten bushels of assorted grains. Despite this crop
failure, however, the Teneycks produced 125 pounds of butter, sold five
dollars worth of chickens, and raised one pig for market. It appears that
they wanted to produce a surplus, evidenced by their effort of plowing
twenty acres of land. But because of poor land, poor weather, or poor
health, they were unable to feed themselves from the produce of their
farm. Perhaps as a result, Robert resorted to carpentry to make ends
meet. Like many others during this period, the Teneycks left their village of Benton in Yates County sometime after 1855. And although we
don't know their ultimate destination, it would seem likely that they
would continue to straddle the agricultural and nonagricultural sectors
of the economy with only modest success in each.[57]

Nonetheless, some farmers with secondary occupations were quite
successful. For example, Daniel Wing, age seventy-four, was originally
from Warren County, New York, but had migrated to the small village
of Ft. Edward in 1811 at the age of thirty. By 1855 Daniel and his wife
apparently had achieved some measure of success. He was listed in the
census as a banker living in an expensive frame home on a twelve-
thousand-dollar farm with two live-in servants. But despite his profes-
sional standing in the community, Daniel maintained his connection to
the soil, harvesting eighteen tons of hay and committing three acres to
the cultivation of winter wheat in 1855. Although his wheat crop failed,
the same cannot be said of this gentleman farmer/banker.[58]

Similarly, William Norton was a successful surplus market farmer and a prominent physician. His two sons, both living at home, were also doctors. Despite Norton's success (the family lived in an expensive home with a servant), they plowed thirty acres of land and harvested a total of 750 bushels of oats, corn, potatoes, and turnips. In addition, they produced 150 pounds of butter, 10 tons of hay, and an assortment of farm animals for both consumption and market.[59]

Thus, many farm families of this period had close connections with the nonagricultural economy. The reasons for their involvement, however, were as varied as their numbers. Some apparently were farmers first, forced to assume secondary occupations to support their families. Others seemed to have been outside the agricultural economy but maintained a small farm to supplement the family diet or to sell dairy products to local townspeople for cash or barter. Still others were successful professionals or skilled workers but also maintained the family farm as a thriving economic unit and regularly produced a surplus for market.

In short, most farmers were involved in the marketplace at some level. And as we will see in the next chapter, differences between farmers who produced a marketable surplus and those who did not partly was a matter of degree. Over the next decade, however, emerging differences in social structure, economic orientation, and world view between them became more pronounced. Indeed, by mid-century most farmers in upstate New York may have looked the same and participated in the marketplace, but they were headed in very different directions both economically and socially.

THE CULTIVATOR,

A MONTHLY PUBLICATION,

DESIGNED TO

IMPROVE THE SOIL AND THE MIND.

CONDUCTED BY J. BUEL, OF ALBANY.

VOLUME V.

ALBANY, N. Y.
FROM THE STEAM PRESS OF PACKARD, VAN BENTHUYSEN & CO.
1838-9.

*The new surplus market farmer in the nineteenth century
turned to a burgeoning agricultural press to
"improve the soil and the mind."*

CHAPTER 5

The Surplus Market Farmer

B y the middle of the nineteenth century, semi-subsistence yeoman and surplus market farmers bore a striking, though superficial, resemblance to one another. Although the latter had greater output in 1855, each was involved (at least occasionally) in the market economy, and typically each employed traditional methods of production based on kin and community cooperation.

Despite these similarities, however, it is also evident that during the decade from 1855 to 1865 differences between these farmers were becoming more pronounced. During these years there was a clear shift toward greater surplus production and increased levels of market involvement. In 1855, just more than half of the sampled New York farmers produced beyond their own food, seed, and stock requirements. By the end of the Civil War, however, about two out of three New York farmers were producing a surplus. In just ten years, then, there was a substantial 14.3 percent increase in the proportion of New York farm families who were part of the surplus market economy.

The magnitude of this shift demonstrates once again that mid-nineteenth-century farm families played a central role in the emergence of the surplus market economy in New York State. Drawn into the web of consumerism and nascent commercial production, these farmers showed the way to future generations of people involved in agribusiness. For better or worse, the agricultural transition toward a more commercialized and consolidated agricultural economy was nearly complete.

This transition was accompanied by the promotion and gradual acceptance of two new ideals regarding the nature of agriculture. The first
was a more scientific, rational, and businesslike approach to farming,
and the second was a "masculinization" of agricultural production. Although New York farmers did not universally embrace these ideals at
mid-century, they represented one end of a spectrum of behaviors and
attitudes, with the more traditional ideals of subsistence farmers at the
other end. Of course, as we have seen, most farmers found themselves
somewhere between these theoretical opposites, balancing traditional
relationships and production methods with rising expectations and a
growing marketplace ethos.

Nevertheless, for the thousands of farmers who wanted to produce
a surplus for market and partake in the growing material culture of the
nineteenth century, the ideals of scientific production and gender specialization were meaningful. And over time, these ideals would come
to distinguish the behavior of surplus market farmers from others.

THE NEW FARMER

As noted in Chapter 1, the agricultural press was in many ways the
"bible" of this new economic order. It was here that the aspiring surplus
market farmer could learn the secrets of increased yields. An early issue of *The Cultivator* reflected some of the new attitudes toward farming that emphasized prudent management of time and energy: "It is as
cheap to raise one ton of grass or clover as a ton of burdocks or pig
weeds."[1]

Careful investment of scarce capital also was seen as a virtue: "A
ten acre field costing fifty dollars per acre ... ditched, manured and improved ... is much more valuable and profitable than twenty acres unimproved ... costing the same money."[2]

But above all, *energy* was the essence of the successful farmer. In
an entertaining article titled "The Sluggish Farmer," the editor of *The
Northern Farmer* noted: "Now reader, if you would know the key to
success in farming, it is *energy* [their italics] and in-domitable perse-
verance that never yields."[3] Indeed, "sluggishness" and laziness could
easily destroy a farmer: "farmers lose money in their business from a

sheer lack of energy to do work at the proper time. They ... are slothful [and] indolent."[4]

By the early 1850s the editor of *The Cultivator* noted an important shift in the attitudes of farmers over the preceding two decades and the critical role the agricultural press had played in that transition: "Then, in 1831, there were but three or four agricultural papers and these had very limited circulation. Farmers had little ambition and their farms with rare exceptions were rapidly deteriorating. Now [in 1851] agricultural papers and books are scattered broadcast over the land, and the demand for information taxes science to its utmost."[5]

The agricultural press clearly was important. As Thomas Cochran has pointed out, the great distances between farms and the lack of communication between farmers during the first three decades of the nineteenth century retarded the development of scientific agriculture. As a result, many American farmers of that period continued to use methods that were typical of the frontier homestead. The land was overcropped, manure was wasted, and ancient methods of tillage and animal production were used.[6]

Of course, some early nineteenth-century farmers understood the ideas of "intensive" scientific agriculture such as deep plowing, crop rotation, the use of calcium fertilizers, and manuring. But without an effective vehicle of communication, these ideas remained exotic to most farmers outside the older commercial agricultural centers clustered along New York's river valleys and adjacent to cities.

The editor of *The Cultivator* understood these problems, and he also knew very well that many farmers were reluctant to engage in what pejoratively was called "book farming." In the December 1851 issue, for example, Luther Tucker noted: "The science of agriculture is yet in its infancy. A mere fraction of the farming population are aroused to the work of improvement."[7]

And yet, these proselytizers were confident that through their instructive articles and personal testimonials of other commercial farmers printed in their pages, a great deal would be done "towards removing existing objections against connecting science with practical agriculture ... and awaken[ing] a spirit of investigation and inquiry."[8]

In fact, by the middle of the century the editor of *The Cultivator* was supremely confident that the ideas of scientific agriculture among the rural population were spreading: "There is no better proof of the rapid progress ... in the improvement of the minds ... of our farmers ... than in the increasing demand for agricultural works both books and journals. ... Our rural population—not perhaps as a body but in large numbers have had their prejudices against 'book farming' dispelled."[9]

Clearly, the agricultural press played a critical role in communicating the ideas of scientific farming. These farming "bibles," published by a cadre of proselytizing rural editors, preached the gospel of soil enrichment and crop rotation with undaunted enthusiasm. They encouraged the systematic application of manures, powdered gypsum (then called plaster of paris), calcium sulfate, and by the 1850s, lime in the form of calcium oxide. They spurned the summer fallow, encouraged the cultivation of red clover or timothy to restore nitrates to the soil, and recommended the occasional return of fields to cattle grazing. Eventually, they embraced the so-called Chester County model as the preferred system throughout the state. It involved the rotation of grains, clover or timothy, grasses, and cattle grazing over a ten-year period. In short, these years witnessed the emergence of a new agriculture and set the stage for the surplus market economy.

THE MASCULINIZATION OF PRODUCTION

As farming gradually was transformed from its rather primitive, semi-subsistence state to a more "rational" enterprise, the agricultural press also promoted vigorously the ideology of "separate spheres." Women were encouraged to leave market production to the menfolk and take up the domestic pursuits of the homemaker and mistress of the orderly farmstead. Once again, while this ideal was seldom fully realized, for many it seemed to be rational behavior based on notions of specialization of labor.

For example, in an article published by *The Northern Farmer* titled "Cheese Making: Process of Manufacturing in Jefferson County," farmer "B" was very clear that dairying, the traditional domain of women, now was man's work: "One simple truth in reference to this subject is quite too much overlooked ... cheese making is a trade [and] an art. ... The trade once learned, a man can hardly entrust his ... dairy to inexperienced and incompetent help. Many of our dairymen make and take care of their own cheese [and] are independent of *very* [his emphasis] uncertain female help and very much relieve their over-burdened 'better halves' of the extra care and labor of keeping a dairy."[10]

Farmer "B" had challenged the traditional patterns of production at mid-nineteenth century, and he knew it. On the one hand he characterized "female help" as very unreliable, but on the other he issued a rather hollow compliment of women being the overburdened better half.

Similarly, the regular appearance of the "Ladies Department" in *The Northern Farmer* and "feminine interest" articles in other farm journals of this period suggests the growing importance these rural editors assigned to the ideology of separate spheres. The "Ladies Department" in the June 1856 issue of *The Northern Farmer* was typical. It began with an essay on night written by "Nellie," who identified herself as a farmer from Seneca County, New York. Next came "A Leaf from my Journal" by "Millie," who argued quite eloquently not to live "alone in the past" but to have faith in the future: "What hour or day is more suited to meditation ... standing as I am on the threshold of another new year." A bit of dark humor followed with a "Letter from an Old Maid" and then a reprinted article from the *Philadelphia Ledger* on tuberculosis and what women could do to prevent it. That month the "Ladies Department" also had two columns of recipes and "helpful tips" for the homemaker. Recipes included baked farina pudding, cinnamon cakes, doughnuts, Lafayette Ginger Cake, and helpful tips to "preserve hams from flies," prevent against moths, and "boil a knuckle of veal" rounded out the column.[11]

The fact that these editors regularly published such "feminine" departments and tips suggests a certain new importance that they had assigned to domestic work and perhaps (at least from their male perspective) a corresponding elevation of its status. At the same time, however, it also is clear that by accepting the ideology of separate spheres, women gradually would lose much of their economic status, which had been based on the shared responsibility of production. Such was the paradox of the emerging "new farm" household in mid-nineteenth-century New York.

Throughout this period Luther Tucker, T.B. Minor, and other rural editors argued forcefully for a scientific approach to agriculture within the context of a strict masculinization of farm production. This division should begin early, they argued, with boys attending to "the out-door affairs and girls to those within."[12]

This "natural" distinction often was presented as a way to protect women from the difficult work of the farm. Women should not be required to "split the wood or carry it into the house, shovel the snow ... carry pails of swill to the hogs or dig potatoes for dinner." Those duties clearly were the "responsibility of the male members of the family."[13]

Husbands often were reminded that the maintenance of this new order was their responsibility. For example, the February 1857 issue of *The Northern Farmer* published an article written by "X" from Clinton, New York, titled "Cheerful Wives." In it, "X" noted that women "may have reason for a little complaint sometimes. The master of the house, has many cares and troubles of which the wife has no conception; and it adds materially to his troubles if his wife meets him with a clouded brow."[14]

And yet were not husbands sometimes responsible for that "clouded brow"? A husband might complain about his wife's flaws, but perhaps he has "furnished [her] with nothing but green wood ... or perhaps the careless lord of creation marches with muddy boots across her well scoured floors, over her well swept carpets and ... [enters the house] with his clothes reeking with the fumes of the barnyard. ... Who is to blame for the wife's clouded brow in this case?"[15]

By attending to their duties, the "lords of creation" could maintain the integrity of this new order and keep their wives as "cheerful as sunbeams, hopeful as children and playful as kittens."[16] Once again, the ideal of separate spheres was clear. According to this article, wives simply had "no conception" of the complex business world. As a result, men must provide them with the material comforts that would keep them satisfied, cheerful, and out of the way.

But while some women were being relieved from the drudgery of digging potatoes and shoveling snow, many men retained more traditional attitudes, beliefs, and behaviors. This was seen as dangerous to the new emerging order of the commercial farming community. In the June 1852 issue of *The Cultivator*, for example, C.H. Cleveland

pleaded with farmers to concern themselves with the material and intellectual wants of their wives and daughters with vigor equal to that
which they applied to meeting the needs of the "hogs and cattle." Before marriage the husband searches for a wife (he wrote) "whose intel-
lect ... has been enlarged and educated to an equal degree with his own.
... Once married however he allows the woman of his love to become
his most devoted slave. From early dawn ... [she will] mend, wash and
sweep and churn, wait upon her husband and his band of laborers, bear
children and nurse them."[17]

And why did husbands revert to those brutish ways? The answer
was simple for Cleveland. The husband had "been accustomed to
see[ing] his neighbors' wives toiling from morning to night." But rather
than applying the same good judgment and rational approach to his
family that he had given to the barnyard, he often succumbed to emu-
late even the most slothful farmer. Cleveland ends his letter by noting
that farmers should not only provide education, recreation, and leisure
for the women in the household, but they should also value their intellectual input, allowing "the females of the family to join with [you] in
forming and executing ... plans for the improvement of the soil and society ... women have a genius above being simply ... maids-of-all-
work."[18]

This shift from physical to intellectual helpmate was a critical aspect of the new rational order, especially as men became more involved
in the increasingly stressful world of the marketplace. As the writer of
one column in the "Ladies Department" of *The Northern Farmer* noted:
"A women has her husband's fortune in her power. When his spirit is
borne down and overwhelmed ... she can minister to his needs. If [he]
is harassed ... her gentle tones [are] more soothing ... than the most ex-
quisite music."[19] And if the crop was a failure, the price of wheat had
plunged, and "if every enterprise be dead ... her patience and fortitude
[can] rekindle them so he can continue with the toils and troubles of
life."[20]

Thus by mid-nineteenth century the powerful ideology of a rational, scientific, market-oriented farm household stratified by gender
with separate spheres assigned to men and women gradually was tak-
ing hold of the consciousness of New York farmers. Men were to dom-

inate all aspects of scientific farm production, and women were expected to maintain the home as a place of beauty, orderliness, and rationality.

Because of this, some New York farm women gradually were relieved of the more onerous tasks of the yeoman household. And the more successful the farming operation, the more convinced farmers became of the efficacy of new scientific agriculture and with it the specialization of production based on gender.

Recently, however, Nancy Grey Osterud has challenged the existence of separate spheres in rural Broome County, New York, in the middle to late nineteenth century. She argues that although gender differentiation within the urban middle class was common by mid-nineteenth century, rural women continued to contribute directly to the production of the household.[21]

Osterud, of course, is correct in pointing to differences between urban and rural women at this time. As demonstrated in Chapter 4, the bridge between semi-subsistence yeomanry and market involvement often was traditional "women's work." Dairying, poultry raising, and miscellaneous household production frequently remained the domain of farm women during this period, and these were the products that found ready markets.

But things gradually were changing. The ideology of separate spheres popularized in the agricultural press was not just an emulation of the urban middle class. It represented the ideal of the scientific commercial farmer and slowly was accepted, sometimes piecemeal, by some farm men and women.

Just as today farm operations vary dramatically, during the middle of the nineteenth century there was also a great deal of variation between farms and regions with regard to production and gender specialization. In dairying communities with access to markets, such as Broome County, more traditional forms of production and gender relations often persisted through the nineteenth century. But even here, as Osterud notes, production varied because of individual tastes. Some women loathed knitting, sewing, and cleaning and preferred to work outdoors whenever they could. Others were "encouraged" through cultural incentives and prohibitions to adopt the separate spheres ideology;

and still others embraced this ideal because they preferred it that way. In this changing social and economic environment, we should expect a variety of behaviors and attitudes operating simultaneously.

Clearly, the mid-nineteenth-century ideology of separate spheres was more than a fantasy of a handful of male rural editors. It was an ideal that many people sought at this time. Some farm families embraced it openly; others did not. Some women welcomed the release from fieldwork and arduous physical labor; others rejected it. But these changes came slowly and most often were intergenerational. A woman who contributed directly to the production of the farm, whose labor was essential to the success of the operation, and whose production often helped realize that elusive surplus would not easily have changed her ways simply because the farm had become successful. Although she might slow down a bit as she aged and take advantage of some of the "geegaws" available to her, we certainly would not expect her to alter fundamentally her work patterns.

The change instead occurred with her daughter or daughter in law—the beneficiary of her lifetime of labor. Osterud's discussion of changes in the work patterns between two generations of Rileys in Broome County illustrates this point. Lucy Ann Riley was a hardworking farm woman. She attended to all the housework, was responsible for the dairy operation (churning, seeing to the milk cows, etc.), and assisted with haying, planting, hoeing, harvesting corn, and digging potatoes. Although there was some mutuality and flexibility in this work, with husband George and son Juddie helping her with churning, washing clothes, and even sewing, it is clear that Lucy Ann was an industrious and productive member of this successful farming enterprise.

However, when son Judson married and brought his bride Lillie into the household, we can see a change. Lillie was unable (perhaps unwilling) to take on all the arduous labor that Lucy Ann had assumed was a natural part of her life. Although Osterud suggests this was because of Lillie's frailty and unfamiliarity with farmwork, it probably also was because of a distinct generational shift in attitudes. Judson "made sure that his wife did not have to work as hard as his mother had done."[22]

Delos Hackley of Batavia, New York (mentioned in Chapter 4), provides us with yet another example of how some farming men at mid-century often crossed the "great gender work divide." Delos tried to make life a little easier for both his mother and later for his "beloved Kate," admitting, throughout his diaries, to helping with the wash, tending the kitchen garden, blackening the stovepipes, choring around, and even sewing on occasion.[23]

Of course, daughters (and sons) of commercial farmers also expected a better life than their parents. Rising expectations of a greater material life also meant less physical work on the farm, and with it often came a tacit acceptance of the ideology of separate spheres. Although mutuality and flexibility of work roles continued throughout the nineteenth and twentieth centuries, the gradual movement toward a separate sphere ideology had taken root in the countryside as it was blossoming in the city.

AGRICULTURAL YIELDS

Whether it was because of a growing acceptance of scientific "book farming," greater specialization of labor, or a combination of both, it is clear that by the end of the Civil War the surplus market farmer in New York State had become very different from the more traditional yeoman. In fact, we will see that their yields of field crops and dairy products, land use, wealth, internal migration, and household organization all distinguished them from the yeoman.[24]

By examining Table 5.1 we can see that from 1855 to 1865 crop yields among New York farmers increased generally. These increases varied by crop. Spring wheat, oats, rye, and peas, for example, declined during the decade. The average pea yield fell 49 percent, while the yield of other crops registered less-dramatic but notable declines. On the other hand, winter wheat, barley, buckwheat, corn, potatoes, beans, and hay all made substantial gains. Thus, although there was a distinct movement toward surplus production among New York farmers during this decade, not all crops were part of this trend.

Table 5.1 also shows that by today's standards, crop yields were

TABLE 5.1
Agricultural Yields and Livestock for 1855 and 1865
(Units per farm recorded in bushels except as noted)

Product	All farmers				Yeomen				Surplus market farmers			
	1855	N	1865	N	1855	N	1865	N	1855	N	1865	N
Field crops												
Spring wheat	25.9	236	17.4	106	14.2	63	9.4	12	30.0	173	18.4	94
Winter wheat	60.9	175	95.6	165	18.9	33	34.1	19	70.7	142	99.3	146
Oats	152.4	572	104.3	560	41.6	170	31.4	102	199.2	402	120.6	458
Rye	60.1	201	53.6	211	31.9	71	30.6	42	75.5	130	59.2	169
Barley	69.5	159	80.4	180	15.7	32	25.4	22	83.0	127	88.0	158
Buckwheat	31.6	320	65.8	309	14.7	104	24.0	36	39.7	216	71.3	273
Corn	85.7	575	100.8	501	28.3	188	31.5	82	113.7	387	114.4	419
Potatoes	78.3	596	131.8	627	41.0	214	67.4	145	99.2	382	151.3	482
Peas	22.7	104	11.5	95	10.5	25	7.8	15	26.5	79	12.1	80
Beans	5.7	43	9.1	87	2.8	16	5.0	18	7.3	27	9.5	69
Hay[a]	13.3	646	19.2	668	5.4	236	5.6	161	19.6	410	25.2	507
Livestock and livestock products												
Dairy cows[b]	8.0	648	11.0	653	4.2	278	5.5	173	11.1	370	13.1	480
Butter[c]	877.6	648	1122.0	653	460.3	278	553.9	173	1217.7	370	1342.8	480
Sheep[b]	9.9	620	17.2	642	3.2	251	3.0	168	15.3	369	23.4	474
Wool[d]	28.6	620	71.5	642	8.2	251	11.5	168	45.1	369	97.8	474

Note: All differences between yeomen and surplus market farmers are significant at the .05 level in both 1855 and 1865 unless noted.
[a]Hay is recorded in tons.
[b]Cows and sheep are recorded as the actual number of animals.
[c]Butter is recorded in pounds.
[d]Wool is recorded in pounds.

very low in mid-nineteenth-century New York. With the exception of oats in 1855 and 1865 and potatoes in 1865, average yields seldom surpassed 100 bushels *per farm*. More typically, grain yields ranged from 25 to 95 bushels per farm, with about 10 to 20 bushels of legumes and 1,300 pounds of butter the norm for surplus producers. In short, crop yields were meager in 1855 but increased during the decade.

YIELDS PER ACRE

What were the typical yields per acre during this period? Until recently, we could not have answered this question for individual farmers at mid-nineteenth century. Although total production figures for field crops were recorded in the U.S. Census after 1850, data on acreage allocated to each crop was not. As a result, agricultural historians have been able to estimate yields of various field crops but have not been able to examine them at the *individual* farm level.

But the records of New York State were different. Cognizant of its growing social, political, and economic importance during this period, the Empire State conducted a statewide agricultural census throughout the nineteenth century in alternate five-year periods from the U.S. Census (1845, 1855, 1865, etc.). Moreover, these censuses were in many ways superior to the federal instruments. For example, acres allocated to each crop were recorded in the 1855 and 1865 New York State agricultural schedules along with the yields for each crop. As a result, we can measure yields per acre for each crop for each New York farm during this period.[25]

Table 5.2 compares the yield figures derived from the linked farmer sample in 1855 and 1865 with Atack and Bateman's regression model estimates and De Bow's mid-nineteenth-century figures. An examination of these data reveals that with some exceptions there was a parallel between these aggregate yield estimates and the figures derived from the 1855 and 1865 New York State censuses. Recognizing the validity of these figures, we are now in a position to move beyond averages to an analysis of individual yields per acre during this period.

Table 5.3 reveals a number of important aspects of agricultural yields in 1855 New York State. First, as expected, it shows that mid-nineteenth-century New York farmers had very small yields by modern

TABLE 5.2
Comparative Yield Estimates at Mid-Nineteenth Century
(Units per acre in bushels except as noted)

Product	1855	1865	DeBow	Atack/Bateman
Spring wheat	9.5	8.5	12.0	11.4
Winter wheat	7.3	9.5	—	—
Oats[a]	19.2	16.5	25.0	27.9
Rye	10.9	11.8	17.0	12.5
Barley	12.2	13.6	25.0	6.9
Buckwheat	8.1	17.5	22.0	7.5
Corn	20.3	23.3	27.0	29.8
Potatoes[b]	63.9	112.1	100.0	12.5
Peas	14.2	10.9	—	3.5
Beans	18.3	11.9	—	(included above)
Hay (in tons)	1.2	0.9	1.1	0.9

Sources: 1855 and 1865 estimates are derived from Parkerson's "linked farmer sample," 1855 and 1865, *New York State Census*. DeBow's estimates are from his compilation of field crop prices. U.S. Census Office, *Statistical View of the United States* (Washington, D.C.: 1854), 178. Atack and Bateman's estimates are regressions of yields in 1860. From *To Their Own Soil* (Ames: Iowa State University Press, 1987), Table 10.3, 170.
[a]Parkerson's 1855 and 1865 yield estimates for oats are slightly below Atack and Bateman's yield range implied by 95 percent confidence interval (19.7-47.1). These estimates are closer to DeBow's estimate.
[b]Parkerson's 1855 and 1865 yield estimates for potatoes are above Atack and Bateman's yield range implied by a 95 percent confidence interval (7.6-34.0). They are, however, in line with DeBow's estimate.

standards. Today, a corn farmer can expect as much as 200 bushels per acre of land in a good year. In 1855, however, grain yields ranged from a state average of about 7 bushels per acre for winter wheat to about 20 bushels per acre for oats and corn. And while New York farmers had better luck with root crops such as potatoes, producing almost 64 bushels per acre in 1855, the yields of peas and beans ranged from a paltry 14 to 18 bushels per acre. In short, today's farmers' yields are between eight to ten times greater than their counterparts' at mid-nineteenth century.

Nevertheless, even with these meager yields, a farm family of six could feed itself by planting just twelve acres of corn or its equivalent. Moreover, a successful harvest from, say, twenty acres of field crops could feed an average farm family as well as one or two additional urban households.

PRODUCTION DIFFERENTIALS

Beneath these figures is another story. As expected, surplus market farmers had much greater yields per farm than others. In 1855 they

TABLE 5.3
Agricultural Yields for 1855 and 1865
(Units per acre except as noted)

Product	All farmers				Yeomen				Surplus market farmers			
	1855	N	1865	N	1855	N	1865	N	1855	N	1865	N
Spring wheat	9.5	236	8.5	106	6.4	63	5.3	12	10.6	173	8.9	94
Winter wheat[a]	7.3	175	9.5	165	3.7	33	10.5	19	8.1	142	9.4	146
Oats	19.2	572	16.5	560	12.4	170	11.7	102	22.0	402	17.6	458
Rye[a]	10.9	201	11.8	211	9.6	71	9.9	42	11.7	130	12.2	169
Barley[a]	12.2	159	13.6	180	6.4	32	13.8	22	13.6	127	13.6	158
Buckwheat	8.1	320	17.5	309	5.4	104	10.8	36	9.4	216	18.4	273
Corn	20.3	575	23.3	501	15.4	188	16.2	82	22.7	387	24.7	419
Potatoes	63.9	596	112.1	627	45.4	214	84.6	145	75.1	382	119.8	482
Peas[a]	14.2	104	10.9	95	9.6	25	11.0	15	15.8	79	10.9	80
Beans[a]	18.3	43	11.9	87	7.3	16	9.1	18	24.9	27	12.2	69
Butter[a,n]	109.7	648	102.0	653	109.6	278	100.7	173	109.7	370	102.5	480
Hay[b]	1.2	646	0.9	668	0.8	236	0.9	161	1.3	410	1.0	507

Note: All differences between yeomen and surplus market farmers are significant at the .05 level in both 1855 and 1865 unless noted.
[a] Butter is recorded in pounds per cow.
[b] Hay is indicated in tons per acre.
[n] Differences between yeomen and surplus market farmers are not significant for butter in either 1855 or 1865. Differences between yeomen and surplus market farmers for winter wheat, rye, barley, peas, and beans are not significant for 1865.

had yields (per farm) that ranged from about twice as great with spring wheat, buckwheat, potatoes, and butter to four or five times as great with oats, corn, and barley (Table 5.1).

We also can see that these farmers had remarkably greater yields per acre than their yeoman neighbors (Table 5.3). These differences sometimes were dramatic. In 1855, for example, surplus market farmers had more than twice the yield per acre of yeomen for barley and winter wheat. And in the case of beans, the yields of the former were more than three times greater than those of yeomen. In fact, surplus market farmers on the whole had nearly 70 percent greater yields than all other farmers in 1855.

Clearly, these farmers often had better land, rotated their crops more often, used manures more intensely, and sometimes experimented with primitive fertilizers such as lime or ash. Moreover, their greater investments in human capital (see Chapter 7) and agricultural tools also helped them improve their yields per farm and acre.

Nevertheless, an aspiring New York yeoman farmer at mid-century could overcome these deficits through dairying. Here, surplus farm families did not have significantly higher yields per cow, although they produced more than twice as much on average (Table 5.1). In 1855 each group produced about 109 pounds of butter per cow. And although market farmers' cows produced slightly more than others in 1865, it is clear that yeomen could compete more successfully in dairying than field crops.[26] In fact, as noted above many of these families were able to produce a surplus by carefully attending to their dairy operations.

The Dutchess, Pitcher, and Robinson households of Yates County mentioned in Chapter 4 illustrate these possibilities. Each of these farm families lived on the margins of the surplus market economy in 1855, and each household head worked in town to supplement his family income. And yet each managed to produce a marketable product (though not a surplus) through the sale of butter and other commodities such as eggs. Moreover, each of these families worked an acre of land (rented), and each raised one cow to produce about one hundred pounds of butter. Through their combined efforts, then, each of these farm households was able to earn a bit of cash and tentatively experiment with the market economy.[27]

By 1865 this picture had begun to change. First of all, while we might have expected a general increase in overall yields per acre by 1865, this was not always the case (Table 5.2). For example, although there was a slight increase in corn, rye, and winter wheat yields per acre, yields for spring wheat and oats were down slightly. On the other hand, buckwheat yields were up substantially (8.1 to 17.5 bushels per acre), as were potatoes (63.9 to 112.1 bushels per acre). In short, changes in agricultural yields were not linear and sometimes varied substantially between crops across the state.

If we compare the per-acre yields of surplus market farmers in 1865 with others, we can see some parallels with 1855 but some surprises as well (Table 5.3). Spring wheat, for example, saw about the same yield differentials in 1865 as in 1855 (about 66 percent). But although surplus market producers had much higher yields than yeomen winter wheat farmers in 1855 (118 percent), these differences virtually had disappeared by 1865. Similarly, there were no significant differentials between the rye, barley, peas, beans, and butter yields of the two groups in 1865. In short, although yields were important keys in understanding the greater production of surplus market farmers in 1855, this factor had become less important by the end of the Civil War.

We might speculate that information on improving yields had become more widespread by 1865 through word of mouth, at state and county fairs, and in the numerous agricultural journals published during the period. Or perhaps it was due to the fact that some unsuccessful yeomen simply had left farming by 1865, thereby decreasing the differential between the two groups. Whatever the reason, it is clear that other factors had become more important by the end of this decade. We must now turn our attention to them.

LAND USE AND FARM AND HOME VALUES

In 1855 landownership among producing farmers (those who appeared in both the agricultural and population schedules of the census, see Appendix 1) was extensive, with nearly 90 percent of those sampled owning some land. By 1865 this figure had grown to a phenomenal 95.8 percent. As expected, then, in both 1855 and 1865 there was no significant difference in landownership between nonsurplus yeomen and surplus market farmers. Among both groups, it had became more widespread during the decade, growing from about 87 to 95 percent among the former and 91 to 96 percent among the latter.

But although levels of landownership increased for these farmers during the decade, the value of their farms did not (Table 5.4). Yeomen farm values declined slightly ($17) in 1865 dollars but plummeted by well over 50 percent in constant 1855 dollars. Surplus market farms, on the other hand, increased in value by about $582 or 14 percent in 1865 dollars, although when we control for wartime inflation, they also declined but much less dramatically. Clearly, the difference in farm values between yeomen and surplus market farms, though substantial in 1855, had become even greater during this period. While surplus farms were assessed at about three times the value of their neighboring yeoman farms in 1855, ten years later they were worth more than four times as much. The same can be said for home values. In 1855 both yeomen and surplus market farmers lived in rather modest dwellings with an average price of about $350. Ten years later, however, things had changed. Surplus market farmers now occupied homes of substantial value ($530 in constant 1855 dollars), whereas the price of a typical yeoman's dwelling declined to $280. This difference was a significant one and indicates both the increasing wealth of surplus market farmers and the growing economic stratification of the agricultural economy by 1865. Once again, while yeoman homes were worth a full 80 percent of the value of their surplus market farming neighbors in 1855, just ten years later their home values had fallen to about one half of that value.

One factor that helps explain these growing differentials was the extent of improved farm acreage. Although this difference was a significant one in 1855, by the end of the decade it had become even more pronounced in terms of both actual acreage per farm and percent differential. For example, in 1855 the average yeoman's farm had 28.3 acres of improved land, increasing just slightly ten years later. Surplus market farmers, on the other hand, either cleared or purchased on average an additional 10 improved acres of land by 1865, from 82.5 to 92.7. Much of this improvement came from the allocation of land to meadow

TABLE 5.4
Land Use, Investments, and Inventories for 1855 and 1865

	All farmers				Yeomen				Surplus market farmers			
	1855	N	1865	N	1855	N	1865	N	1855	N	1865	N
Land use												
Improved acres	58.2	777	73.5	738	28.3	348	29.7	225	82.5	429	92.7	513
Unimproved acres	38.2	777	33.4	738	30.5	348	24.4	225	44.5	429	37.3	513
Percent improved	60.4	777	68.7	738	48.1	348	54.8	225	64.9	429	71.3	513
Meadow acres	16.0	777	21.3	738	7.6	348	8.3	225	22.9	429	27.0	513
Plowed acres	15.6	777	14.5	738	7.1	348	4.6	225	22.5	429	18.8	513
Investments and inventories (in dollars)[a]												
Home	357	777	645 (463)	738	311	348	438 (280)	225	385	429	726 (530)	513
Farm	2898	777	3694 (2216)	738	1354	348	1327 (636)	225	4151	429	4733 (2616)	513
Implements	103	777	166 (113)	738	55	348	54 (26)	225	143	429	215 (142)	513
Stock	380	777	547 (353)	738	191	348	217 (120)	225	533	429	691 (419)	513

Note: All differences between yeomen and surplus market farmers are significant at the .05 level in both 1855 and 1865 unless noted.
[a]Values in parentheses are expressed in constant 1855 dollars to control for inflation.

or pasture. Surplus farmers typically increased their meadow by 4 or 5 acres, with yeoman adding only about 1 acre to meadow for hay (Table 5.4). And although there are no comparable data for 1855, surplus market farmers increased their allocation of land to pasture by more than an acre on average, from 31.4 to 32.5 acres in just one year (1864–65).

One of the many examples of this trend was the Lyman Hull household of Durham Township, Greene County, New York. In 1855 the Hulls produced below surplus even though their farm size was substantial. By 1865, however, they successfully had produced a surplus, in part because they had been able to clear and improve an additional 42 acres of land. This allowed them to increase their field crop cultivation slightly from 18 to 22 acres and their pasturage significantly from 47 to 70 acres. They then invested in sheep, nearly tripling their wool production from 160 to 450 pounds, and more than doubled their production of field crops from about 160 to 388 bushels. For the Lyman Hulls, as with many mid-nineteenth-century commercial farm households, one key to producing a market surplus was improving as much available land as possible and then placing it in pasture or meadow. In fact, by 1865 surplus market farmers like the Hulls were living on farms that were more than 70 percent improved, whereas yeomen had improved only about 54 percent of their land (Table 5.4).[28]

While surplus market farmers improved more land during this decade, they also invested some of their profits in agricultural tools of all kinds (Table 5.4). Across the state, surplus market farmers increased their inventories of implements by an average of $72 ($143 to $215). This represented an overall increase of more than 50 percent, although when we control for the temporary effect of wartime inflation, the value appears to have stayed about the same. Tool inventories of yeoman farmers, on the other hand, declined dramatically (in constant 1855 dollars). As a result, by the end of the Civil War, the tool inventories of surplus market farmers were more than five times as great as those of yeomen. Clearly, they were investing in their future production and aggressively seeking profits from the new markets that had emerged during the war years.

An examination of several farmers who made the transition to surplus market production during this decade illustrates the importance of

this kind of investment. Lyman Hull, Levi Gilbert, John Hull, and
Jonah Ransom, all of Greene County, produced below surplus in 1855.
By 1865, however, each had managed a surplus. John made this transition while still in his twenties, Lyman in his thirties, Jonah in his forties, and Levi in his fifties. One common thread to their commercial
success was their investment in agricultural tools. With the exception
of Jonah Ransom, each farmer doubled his investment to two hundred
or three hundred dollars by 1865. And while Jonah Ransom increased
his tool inventory only slightly by the end of the decade, the census revealed that he took three young male relatives into his household who
presumably helped out. Similarly, Levi Gilbert both extended his
household and invested in agricultural tools.[29]

Nevertheless, we should not exaggerate the importance of these
investments. Although two hundred dollars was a substantial amount of
capital, it did not allow for significant mechanization of the farm. The
seventy-two dollar increase in tool inventories among commercial
farmers during this decade would upgrade some existing implements,
from, say, a wooden to an iron plow, a hand-made wagon to a manufactured one, or a wooden harrow to one made of iron. But these farms
were hardly mechanized, even by the standards of the day. Moreover,
if the farmer made these purchases during the hyperinflation of
1864–65, these increases barely would have kept pace with rising
prices. As a result, it appears that investments in human capital like
those made by Jonah Ransom were often just as important.

The greater yields of surplus market farmers, then, were partly due
to their improvement of land, especially for meadow and pasturage, as
well as their modest upgrading of agricultural implements. With these
strategies, surplus producers were able to capitalize more fully on new
opportunities brought about by the Civil War.

LAND ALLOCATION

How was land used in mid-nineteenth-century New York? Once
again, we can see some important changes between 1855 and 1865, the
most striking of which was a shift from grain production to dairying
and sheep raising. Table 5.4 shows that during these years the cultiva-

tion of grain crops actually declined slightly among surplus market farmers, whereas their dairy and wool production increased sharply.

In 1855 New York surplus market farmers typically plowed 22.5 acres and yeomen only 7.1 acres. By 1865, however, these figures had dropped slightly for the former to 18.8 acres (a 16 percent decline), with yeomen farmers plowing only 4.6 acres (a decline of more than 34 percent).

As mentioned above, the allocation of land to meadow increased sharply during the decade. Although all New York farmers allocated only 16 acres of land to meadow in 1855, more than 21 acres were in meadow ten years later. Moreover, most of this increase came from surplus market farmers, who increased their meadow allocation from 22 to 27 acres on average, an increase of more than 17 percent.

Finally, an examination of livestock values reveals that by 1865 the typical surplus market farmer owned more than three times as much livestock as the yeoman (Table 5.4). Even when we consider the effect of wartime inflation, these differences are impressive ($419 versus $120).

Surplus market farmers typically led the way once again. By 1865 they registered an increase in their numbers (to 94 percent) who produced butter (Table 5.5) and increased their dairy cattle by about two cows on average (11.1 to 13.1 cows; see Table 5.1). Similarly, surplus market farmers increased their production of hay by 29 percent (19.6 to 25.2 tons per farm; see Table 5.1) in just ten years. The increase in wool production was even more pronounced, with surplus farmers more than doubling their wool production from about 45 pounds to nearly 98 pounds (Table 5.1). Moreover, as Table 5.5 demonstrates, the percentage of surplus market farmers producing grains declined, with only a few exceptions.

Faced with growing competition from grain producers farther west, many New York farmers shifted their production to dairying and wool. This shift was even more dramatic among surplus market farmers, who apparently understood well the importance of regional market specialization and the production niche that New York State had come to occupy in the economy.

Moreover, as suggested above, dairying and wool production

TABLE 5.5
Percentage of Farmers Producing Various Products for 1855 and 1865

Product	All farmers				Yeomen				Surplus market farmers			
	1855	N	1865	N	1855	N	1865	N	1855	N	1865	N
Spring wheat	30.3	236	14.4	106	18.1	63	5.3	12	40.3	173	18.4	94
Winter wheat	22.5	175	22.4	165	9.5	33	8.4	19	33.1	142	28.6	146
Oats	73.6	572	76.0	560	48.9	170	45.1	102	93.7	402	89.6	458
Rye	25.9	201	28.6	211	20.4	71	18.6	42	30.3	130	33.1	169
Barley	20.5	159	24.4	180	9.2	32	9.7	22	29.6	127	30.9	158
Buckwheat	41.2	320	41.9	309	29.9	104	15.9	36	50.3	216	53.2	273
Corn	74.0	575	68.0	501	54.0	188	36.3	82	90.2	387	82.0	419
Potatoes	76.6	596	85.0	627	61.5	214	64.2	145	89.0	382	94.3	482
Peas	13.4	104	12.9	95	7.2	25	6.6	15	18.4	79	15.7	80
Beans	5.5	43	11.8	87	4.6	16	8.0	18	6.3	27	13.5	69
Butter	83.4	648	88.6	653	79.9	278	76.5	173	86.2	370	94.0	480
Hay	83.1	646	90.6	668	67.8	236	71.2	161	95.6	410	99.2	507

Note: All differences between yeomen and surplus market farmers are significant at the .05 level in both 1855 and 1865 unless noted.

offered a "dual incentive." Not only were these profitable enterprises, but they allowed New York farmers to enter the surplus marketplace without completely abandoning traditional forms of production. The Levi Gilbert household mentioned above made this sort of transition while Levi was in his late fifties. Part of their production strategy, it appears, was an upgrading of their agricultural tools as well as the extension of their household with two relatives who presumably assisted with their expanding dairy and sheep raising operations. In 1855 the Gilberts produced eight tons of hay and had two cows producing two hundred pounds of butter.

By 1865 they had produced thirty-five tons of hay and increased their meadow acreage from twelve to seventy-seven acres! By the end of the decade, they had twenty cows producing 2000 pounds of butter and 150 pounds of cheese for market. The Gilberts also moved vigorously into sheep and wool production during this period, breeding a substantial flock of 113 sheep (they had none in 1855) and an additional 50 lambs in 1865 alone. In fact, they doubled their livestock holdings to nearly fifteen hundred dollars by the decade's end. While the Gilberts continued to plow ten to fifteen acres of land for field crops, the family's shift to dairying and wool production, like so many others during this period, was remarkable.[30]

These land-use and wealth comparisons tell us a great deal about the nature of agriculture in mid-nineteenth-century New York State and by inference something of northern agriculture in general. First, they reveal increasing levels of landownership among sampled New York household heads during this period. Second, they show that wealth stratification (as suggested by farm and dwelling values) had begun to accelerate by the end of the Civil War. Overall, farm values increased sharply in 1865 dollars during this decade for surplus market farmers but stalled or declined for yeomen. After controlling for inflation, one can see a general decline, with the latter's farm values falling dramatically. Third, surplus market farmers aggressively sought to capitalize on new market opportunities during the Civil War. They improved their land (most significantly for meadow), upgraded their agricultural implements, moved aggressively into dairying and wool production, and, as we will see in Chapter 7, increased their human capital by extending their households with working relatives. The typical yeoman farming household, on the other hand, did not clear additional land, invest in new agricultural tools, move into dairying and sheep raising, or alter significantly its household organization to improve human capital.

The investments and production strategies of surplus market farmers had increased their yields and made them wealthier by 1865. The long-term effects of these changes were profound and would be felt for the rest of the nineteenth century. The mechanisms that would spawn a more stratified, consolidated, commercial agricultural economy clearly were in place by the summer of 1865. The agricultural transition was nearly complete.

*A dynamic farm community might have fairs and
expositions at which new farming implements
could be seen and ideas exchanged.*

CHAPTER   6

Migration, Markets, and Mobility

We have seen that mid-nineteenth-century New York was being transformed by powerful forces of urbanization, industrialization, and the emergence of the surplus market economy. Paralleling these changes was a dramatic rise of the internal migration of people. A new culture of mobility had begun to permeate the social and economic life of the state and the nation as a whole.

But what were the relationships between internal migration, market opportunity, and the agricultural transition? Were migrants the passive victims of a rapidly changing rural economy? Or were they active agents of change whose voluntary movement restructured New York's human capital for greater productivity and economic growth? In Chapter 2 we saw that each of these images has been firmly entrenched in the historical literature. For progressive historians and functionalist sociologists, migrants were a diaspora of helpless victims of an economy in turmoil. Migration in their view was a reflection of fundamental problems of economic organization. Frontier historians, on the other hand, typically perceived migrants in more positive terms. For these scholars migrants were dynamic individuals who took advantage of the great economic opportunities available to Americans of all walks of life.

Here we have two well-developed models that describe the migrant, each designed to illustrate a particular world view. In both models, however, the migrant is not a central actor in the unfolding historical drama but simply grist for the mill of a particular historical vision.

As we have seen, migration was a much more complex process than either of these models suggests, and the migrant was in fact both a victim and an active agent of change during this period.

What, then, was the nature of the relationship between migration and the commercial agricultural economy? Tables 6.1 and 6.2, which show the percentage of persisting, in-migrating, and out-migrating farmers producing a surplus in 1855 and 1865, provide some answers. Each migration group also is examined by the section of the state in which they lived.

An examination of Table 6.1 indicates that although residentially stable persisters on the whole were more likely to have produced a surplus in both 1855 and 1865, many mid-nineteenth-century New York farmers also used internal migration as a vehicle to enter the surplus market economy. Despite the great difficulties associated with moving, it appears that migrating farmers committed themselves to surplus market farming just as aggressively.

For example, this analysis shows that out-migrants were not always poor semi-subsistence farmers buffeted about the state by the forces of economic change (Table 6.2). Many were small-scale surplus market farmers attempting to improve their lot through internal migration. Certainly, their substantial involvement in that economy, although lower than more established (persisting) farmers in the state, indicates that many of them had moderate wealth and presumably were trying to "make it" in a rapidly changing agricultural economy.

Hiram Odell, age forty-six, was typical of this type of farmer. Hiram and his wife arrived in Broome County as newlyweds in 1838, and over the next seventeen years they raised six children and established a rather substantial farm of nearly 130 acres worth thirty-seven hundred

TABLE 6.1
Migration, Section, and Surplus Production 1855 and 1865
(Percentage producing a surplus)

| | Persisters between 1855 and 1865 | | | |
	1855	N	1865	N
Section				
Hudson River Valley	62.3	207	80.2	207
Adirondacks, Allegheny	42.9	56	64.3	56
Erie Canal corridor	72.8	92	77.2	92

TABLE 6.2
Migration, Section, and Surplus Production for 1855 and 1865
(Percentage producing a surplus)

	Migrants between 1855 and 1865			
	Out-migrants	N	In-migrants	N
Section				
Hudson River Valley	53.6	125	70.0	120
Adirondacks, Allegheny	32.3	164	44.9	98
Erie Canal corridor	63.8	127	82.7	150

dollars. By 1855 they had diversified their production, raising sheep, swine, and cows; planting 40 acres of assorted grains for market; and allocating another 25 acres to meadow. Having achieved a degree of success, the Odells, like thousands of others, out-migrated during the decade, perhaps to take advantage of even greater opportunities elsewhere.[1]

Although neither the ultimate destination nor future achievements of the Odells can be determined in this study, we can infer their fate as well as that of other out-migrants by examining the fortunes of in-migrants to New York communities. After all, every out-migrant also was a recent in-migrant.

An examination of in-migrants in 1865 shows that many successfully had produced a surplus by that year (Table 6.2). The most productive were those who moved to growing commercial communities along the Erie Canal, where more than 80 percent were able to produce a surplus for market. This level of involvement in surplus production was even greater than that of persisting farmers anywhere in the state. In short, growing market communities attracted many migrant farmers who clearly were oriented toward surplus production and the cash economy associated with it.

William Skillie of Argyle Township in Washington County was one such farmer. William and his young wife in-migrated to Argyle sometime after 1855, and with the help of his co-resident father-in-law and brother-in-law, they were able to participate in the surplus market economy with remarkable success. The Skillie farm was not enormous by the standards of the day—only 160 acres—but they used their land intensively. All but 30 acres had been improved, with 40 under field crop cultivation, 30 in pasture, and another 25 allocated to meadow.

Their $750 investment in agricultural implements and tools by the summer of 1865 also was substantial, far above the mean of commercial farmers across the state. Moreover, their output was diverse; they harvested oats, rye, buckwheat, potatoes, beans, corn, and flax, with their thirty-tree orchard yielding two hundred bushels of apples and six barrels of cider. Finally, their $700 of livestock included dairy cows producing 400 pounds of butter, pigs yielding 1500 pounds of pork, a substantial flock of sheep producing about 250 pounds of wool, and an additional $100 in poultry. The Skillies therefore were not the flotsam and jetsam of New York rural society but rather aggressive, market-oriented farmers who had in-migrated to Washington County to take advantage of commercial opportunities in the area.[2]

Migration could and often did make a difference. While not all migrants were as successful as stable persisting farmers, their production was often remarkable considering their recent arrival in their communities. If a migrant farm family understood the nature of opportunities in the state, if they had the necessary capital to make the move, and if they had the requisite familial connections at their ultimate destination, they had a good chance of competing successfully in the surplus commercial economy.

As might be expected, however, long-distance lifetime migration (interstate or international) often was a barrier to one's entry into surplus market production. The enormous difficulties and high costs associated with moving long distances typically worked against these farmers in terms of producing a surplus for market. The more successful of these migrants either remained in their communities after their move, or better yet, they chose areas that offered the greatest market opportunities as their settlement destinations. In this way many uprooted mid-nineteenth-century migrant farmers could tentatively and quite often successfully venture into surplus market production. In fact, more than half (51.4 percent) of the European immigrants who persisted during this decade had become surplus producers by 1865, as did nearly seven in ten (69.6 percent) of the interstate migrants.

Other long-distance migrants did not fare as well, though it must be remembered that not all of these farmers had planned to produce a surplus product. The primary ambition for many of them was landownership and perhaps occasional market involvement. These goals very often were achieved by migrants of all sorts.

THE GAMBLE OF MIGRATION

Although migration often was associated with successful entry into the world of surplus market production, the road was fraught with peril. To get some sense of these difficulties, I examined court-ordered farm repossessions in Lewis County, New York, following the panic of 1857. I then linked these documents to the manuscript population and agricultural schedules of the 1855 New York State Census to determine social and economic positions. And since the 1855 New York State Census recorded information on the continuous years of residence of each household member, I could assess the relationship between migration and bankruptcy.

As expected, the migrant and not the stable resident was the most economically vulnerable. Of the thirty-two families whose farms were repossessed and recorded by Sheriff S.G.E. Wentworth in the months immediately following the panic of 1857, only five were natives of the county. In fact, it appears that the probability of bankruptcy increased sharply among very recent arrivals to Lewis County. Of the twenty-seven migrant bankruptcies recorded, twenty-one were filed on farmers who arrived in their communities between June of 1855 and June of 1857. In short, although internal migration could be a powerful vehicle by which New York farmers could achieve upward economic mobility through involvement in the surplus market economy, it was also a gamble that could turn sour and lead to financial ruin.[3]

The John Malloy household provides a good example of these difficulties. He and his wife Mary had moved from St. Lawrence County to Lewis County in 1853, settling in a small frame home on a farm valued at thirteen hundred dollars. Their farm was of substantial size, though underdeveloped, with only nineteen improved acres and another ninety-three acres of woodland where the family harvested maple syrup in the spring of 1855. In that year the Malloys owned one hundred dollars worth of livestock and had invested fifty dollars in agricultural implements. Although not successful surplus commercial farmers, John and his family clearly were part of the occasional market economy, raising chickens for sale and harvesting more than eleven tons of hay.

Then in the spring of 1857 their finances went foul, and the Malloys were unable to pay their debts. As a result, the sheriff swiftly repossessed all their land, which later was auctioned. Although the Malloys were recent in-migrants, they were not total strangers to their community. In fact, their farm was adjacent to that of a brother, Thomas Malloy, who apparently was unable to help out during this financial crisis.[4]

Nicholas Smith of Osceola Township, Lewis County, provides us with yet another example of the risks of migration in the context of market involvement. Nicholas, age forty-six in 1855, was originally from Rhode Island, and like many farmers during this period he worked outside of agriculture to supplement the household income. The Smith's owned seventy-five acres of land in 1855, and that year they harvested a small amount of corn and potatoes as well as more than fifty pounds of maple syrup from their seventy-three acres of unimproved land.

But despite the Smith's apparently secure, semi-subsistence lifestyle, they too ran into financial difficulties in 1857 and were unable to pay back a $350.32 debt to William Rowell. As a result, three days after Christmas in 1857 the sheriff appeared at their door and seized their farm. A few months later in March of 1858 it was auctioned and purchased by Rowell for less than half its assessed value.[5]

While John Malloy and Nicholas Smith were producing just below surplus with some occasional market involvement, migrant surplus market farmers with considerable wealth and yields also were vulnerable to the vagaries of the economic cycle. Such was the case of thirty-five-year-old William Royce. William, his wife Emma, and their six children had migrated to Lewis County from Jefferson County sometime in 1854. The Royces then purchased a three thousand dollar farm consisting of 150 acres of improved land and proceeded to invest in both stock and implements. By June of 1855 they had become very successful. They had twenty working cows that produced more than twenty-seven hundred pounds of butter for market, and they had plowed 42 acres of land with another 94 in pasture. Their field crop output, moreover, was substantial, with more than eleven hundred bushels of assorted grains and twelve tons of hay that year.

By the end of 1858, however, tragedy descended on the Royce household. Apparently strapped financially, they were unable to repay a small debt of $224.38 to one Roswell Sherman. As a result, on November 2 of that year, after the harvest, Deputy Sheriff Dagitt seized their farm, livestock, and implements. Thus, for the lack of just over $200 in cash, the Royces lost their farm and ended, at least temporarily, their brief career in commercial farming. Clearly, market involvement was risky business, and when compounded by the vulnerability of migration, it was even riskier.[6]

MARKET ECOLOGIES

Despite this gamble, migration often was associated with successful surplus market involvement in mid-nineteenth-century New York. Perhaps as suggested above, the very act of migration promoted a sense of pragmatism and entrepreneurship. Or perhaps migration was self-selective, with only those with extraordinary motivation actually moving. Whatever the case, the migrant's choice of a destination was equally important in determining success or failure. By examining market access in the context of migration, we can begin to understand more fully both the shift to a surplus market economy and the central role migration played in that transition.

Figure 6.1 is a theoretical array of communities according to their volume of both in- and out-migration, and Figure 6.2 represents the plot of mid-nineteenth-century New York rural communities. By examining Figure 6.2 we can see a number of community clusters. For the sake of conceptual clarity, the inverse of the persistence rate was used as an estimate of out-migration, and years of continuous residence in a community was used as a proxy for in-migration. Since the persistence rate is a measure of the percentage of individuals who remained in the community for ten years, its inverse (100 minus persistence rate) is a good proxy for out-migration. Moreover, since recent in-migrants to the community had a short duration of residence, the lower the mean of this variable, the greater the in-migration to that community. Of course, these measures are far from perfect. But they do provide us with a unique perspective on the simultaneous processes of in- and out-migration and allow us to examine these processes in the context of agricultural change.

An examination of these community clusters suggests a general topology of migration archetypes, what might be called "market ecologies." Communities experiencing high in-migration coupled with low out-migration were classified as "dynamic." "Stable" communities, on the other hand, also had low out-migration, but few people in-migrated to these areas. Transitional "marginal" communities exhibited rapid population turnover, with both high in- and out-migration. Finally, "exit" communities had relatively low in-migration and high levels of out-migration.

These market ecologies represent the cumulative effect of historical, demographic, and economic development in New York State during the first half of the nineteenth century. With only a few exceptions, there is a close relationship among a community's physical location in the state, market access, and corresponding migration profile cluster. Typically, counties located along the Hudson River Valley were stable, such as Greene and Washington counties; those located along the Erie Canal corridor were dynamic, such as Erie and Monroe counties; and those in the rugged Adirondack Mountains, the Catskills, and the Allegheny Plateau in the southern tier of the state were marginal. In short,

FIGURE 6.1
Ecological Level Perspectives on Migration (market ecologies)

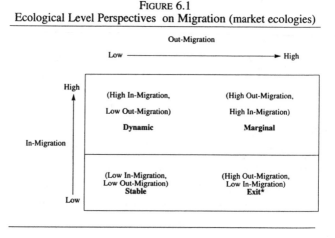

*Not extant in mid-nineteenth-century New York.

FIGURE 6.2
Market Ecologies

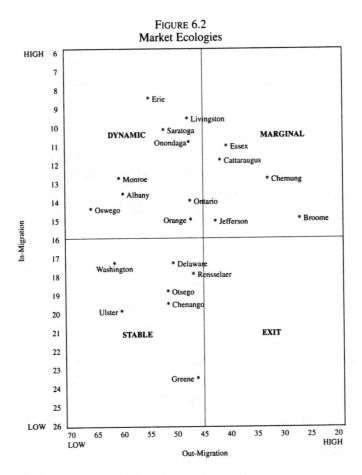

what we have identified here is an association between ecological patterns of migration, geographic location, historical development, and the development of the surplus market economy.[7]

DYNAMIC ECOLOGIES

By examining Figure 6.2 again, we can see the general clustering of New York counties into three of the four sectors of this array. The first cluster, dynamic ecologies, were economically viable and flourishing. As a result, many people settled in these areas and relatively few left once they arrived.

Ansel Cushman, his wife, and eight children, apparently recognized the opportunities in dynamic Saratoga County and in 1854 moved to the area. The Cushmans were just one of thousands of households that streamed into dynamic growth areas like Saratoga during this period.[8] Charles Murray, forty-four, also may have sensed these opportunities and in 1835 at the age of twenty-four had migrated from Connecticut with his wife Mary and settled in booming Monroe County near Rochester. As a carpenter and part-time farmer, Charles took part in the great building boom in and around that city which had been spurred by the construction of the Erie Canal in the early 1820s. By 1855 Charles and Mary had done very well for themselves and were living in an impressive twenty-five hundred dollar home with their three children and a young female servant from New Jersey.[9]

Immigrants also streamed into dynamic growth communities during this period. Gilbert Jones was a recent in-migrant from Germany who settled in Monroe County in late 1852. His commitment to the community seemed clear because by June of 1855 he had acquired some land and married Elizabeth, a native New Yorker. As a skilled machinist and occasional market farmer, Gilbert benefited from the thriving economy of this region and in 1855 was listed in the census as occupying an impressive brick home with his new wife and child.[10]

By examining Table 6.3 we can see that surplus farmers in dynamic ecologies also did well for themselves and typically experienced a marked increase in their net agricultural production. These farm households were capable of feeding themselves and three or four additional adults for a year in 1855, but that number grew to nearly eleven adults by the end of the Civil War. This represented an actual increase of nearly three hundred additional bushels of corn equivalents per farm family or a 201 percent increase in net production in just ten years (Table 6.3).

STABLE ECOLOGIES

Like dynamic areas, stable market ecologies also had high persistence (low out-migration), but these communities attracted fewer new residents, as indicated by their higher average continuous years of res-

TABLE 6.3
Yields by Market Ecology for 1855 and 1865

Market ecology	1855			1865			1855 to 1865	
	Yield	N	Feeds	Yield	N	Feeds	Inc.	% Inc.
Dynamic (Erie Canal corridor)	146.2	237	3.6	440.1	272	10.7	239.9	201.0
Stable (Hudson River Valley)	184.7	326	4.5	648.9	318	15.8	464.2	251.1
Marginal (Adirondacks, Allegheny)	20.9	214	0.5	67.5	151	1.6	46.4	223.0

Note: Yield represents the average number of bushels of corn equivalents produced beyond farm requirements and human consumption needs. Feeds represents the average number of additional adult males (beyond the farm family) that farmers were capable of feeding per year. Inc. represents the average increase in net bushels of corn equivalents produced during the decade. % Inc. represents the percentage increase during the period.

idence (a lower level of in-migration). These communities had reached a kind of economic equilibrium. Their economies could support their current population well, but there were fewer new opportunities for outsiders. Often located in older commercial regions along the Hudson, Mohawk, or other river valleys, these stable ecologies had great economic viability and thus were able to retain their resident populations. But the few new opportunities discouraged large-scale in-migration.

Most of these communities were settled early in the state's history, and the typical pattern of residence was long-term intergenerational persistence. William Gibson, age fifty-eight, was in some ways typical. In 1836 at the age of thirty-six he moved to the town of Argyle in Washington County on the upper Hudson, bought a farm, and remained there for the rest of his life.[11] Argyle was a characteristic stable commercial town. It was settled in 1742 and grew slowly over the next hundred years, reaching a peak of about three hundred people.[12] From then on, its population remained almost unchanged. But despite its "sleepy" demographic appearance, it flourished economically. Most farmers living in Argyle at mid-century had successfully entered the surplus market economy and remained in that town their entire lives. More often than not, they transferred their wealth to the next generation, who then would persist residentially.

As expected, many farmers in these communities did extremely well during this period, with the greatest net yields in the state in 1855 (Table 6.3). By 1865 these farmers had increased their net output by an astounding 464.2 bushels of corn equivalents. In fact, the average farm family in these communities was capable of producing enough food for nearly sixteen adults beyond their own needs.

Simon Crandall was typical in this regard. He arrived in Washington County in 1839 at the age of twenty-three. Over the next decade and a half, he and his wife raised five children and worked a small farm of sixty-eight acres. In 1855 the Crandalls had achieved moderate success, plowing twenty-one acres of land and harvesting nearly one thousand bushels of corn, buckwheat, winter wheat, and oats. Although they did have four working oxen, the Crandalls were "stock poor," with no horses, cattle, swine, or sheep. By 1865, however, things had changed. Simon, now forty-nine years old, his wife, and five grown children were still living on the homestead. Together, they nearly tripled their farm size and doubled their improved acreage. Moreover, the value of their farm quadrupled to $11,000 and their tool inventory tripled to $450, well above the state average. The Crandalls continued to produce about one thousand bushels of assorted cereal grains for market, but now they were committed to animal husbandry. Here their increase was enormous. Like many other farm families in the highly developed commercial region of the Hudson, the Crandall's recognized the growing demand for meat, poultry, and especially dairy products. As a result, they directed much of their capital and energy to developing this aspect of their farm. They established a dairy with fifteen cows that produced 700 pounds of butter and 50 pounds of cheese for market. They also raised fifty-six sheep in 1865 (up from thirty-six in 1864) and sold 280 pounds of wool. Similarly, they produced 2400 pounds of pork and raised five horses. Overall, their stock holdings increased nearly fivefold, from $355 in 1855 to $1500 in 1865. Clearly, the Crandalls understood the emerging markets of New York very well. They also recognized the rapidly changing structure of northern commercial agriculture and the special niche that farmers along the Hudson River Valley had come to occupy.[13]

MARGINAL ECOLOGIES

Marginal market ecologies were by far the most residentially unstable and were characterized by relatively high levels of both in- and out-migration. These communities typically were located in areas with emerging markets and rapidly changing opportunities. The transient William Wort and his family, introduced in Chapter 2, was in many ways characteristic of the kinds of individuals who streamed into, around, and sometimes out of these marginal market communities during this period. In 1855 the Worts were recent in-migrants to Jefferson County, though an examination of the birthplaces of the Wort children demonstrates that the family had migrated at least five times between Jefferson and Oswego counties since 1837.[14] Perhaps in their life-long search for success the Worts were attracted to what one observer called the "sandy loam [soil] of a superior quality and ... abundant crops" of Jefferson County.[15] Or perhaps they knew that even if they were unable to make it in the surplus commercial economy, William could supplement the family income as a sawyer in this abundant timber region. Whatever their reasons, the Worts recently had moved to this community and were living in a small log cabin with an estimated value of only five dollars. By 1865 they apparently had moved on. Clearly, their search for economic security was not over.

On the other hand, N.G. Clark, a doctor, was born and raised in a marginal agricultural ecology but out-migrated, perhaps because he recognized greater opportunities elsewhere. Clark was originally from Steuben County. In 1844 at the age of thirty-five he left home and traveled north, probably on the old Ridge Road, to Clarkson Village in Monroe County located eighteen miles west of thriving Rochester. In 1840 Clarkson had a population of just under thirty-four hundred, but the town grew rapidly and later would become part of the Rochester metropolitan complex. Clark apparently had made the right move because by 1855 he was living in a four thousand dollar frame mansion with his wife, Grace, three children, and two servants.[16] Whatever their varied reasons, thousands of New Yorkers moved into and sometimes out of these marginal market communities, often searching for just the right place to settle.

As expected, marginal market ecologies like those located in the Adirondacks and Allegheny Plateau were dominated by semi-subsistence yeomen who had only occasional market involvement. In fact, only a handful of the farmers in these communities actually had produced a surplus for market during this decade. Those who had, however, serviced the local markets of the growing towns in the region. In

1855 the typical farm household in these sorts of communities had not produced a surplus for market; the average farm yielded only 21 bushels of corn equivalents beyond bare subsistence (Table 6.3). By 1865 these farmers had slightly higher yields of 67.5 net bushels of corn or about enough to feed one adult and one small child for a year beyond their own needs.

EXIT ECOLOGIES

The final market type in this model is theoretical, but if it existed it might be called an exit ecology. Communities of this sort would be characterized by both low in-migration and high out-migration (Figure 6.1). As might be expected, none of the mid-nineteenth-century upstate communities fit this category. Exit ecologies had declining economic opportunities that encouraged significant out-migration but offered few new opportunities to encourage in-migration. Similar to some of Hal Barron's New England towns, exit communities were victims of economic change and growing opportunities elsewhere.[17] By the twentieth century, however, a number of previously thriving New York communities would have moved into the exit category.

THE TRANSFORMATION OF THE AGRICULTURAL ECONOMY: 1855–65

Each of these market ecologies exhibited a distinct pattern of migration that corresponded to a general level of commercial development. By examining each of these ecologies within a multivariate framework, we can begin to appreciate the complex transformation of the agricultural economy during this decade. Table 6.4 presents the regression analysis of net yields with migration (persistent or not), farm characteristics, age, the dollar value of the farm, and other factors. This table also presents analyses for each market ecology in both 1855 and 1865.

When we examine each market ecology separately, the effect of persistence disappears for the most part. Whether a farmer was a persister in either 1855 or 1865 did not have a significant relationship to net yields once other factors were considered. Although persisters did have greater net yields in 1865 (note the nonsignificant b-values, espe-

TABLE 6.4
Regression of Net Yields by Market Ecology for 1855 and 1865

	1855			1865		
	Stable	Marginal	Dynamic	Stable	Marginal	Dynamic
Persistence	−13.463	−41.140	−10.781	291.169	22.721	61.018
	(−0.49)	(−1.42)	(−0.35)	(1.01)	(0.70)	(0.74)
Age	−0.401	−0.899	−3.530*	−5.775	−0.150	−3.290
	(−0.39)	(−0.77)	(−2.84)	(−0.49)	(−0.12)	(−0.96)
Home value	−0.034	−0.029	0.004	0.314	0.009	−0.037
	(−1.22)	(−0.62)	(0.09)	(1.38)	(0.29)	(−0.60)
Farm value	−0.015	0.027*	0.009	0.041*	0.022*	0.042*
	(−0.05)	(1.88)	(0.89)	(1.98)	(2.95)	(1.87)
Acres plowed	6.691*	8.482*	5.155*	30.710*	11.287*	16.434*
	(6.05)	(5.09)	(3.55)	(2.43)	(5.89)	(3.63)
Acres meadow	0.878	3.44*	−0.364	5.001	5.270*	1.154
	(1.29)	(1.80)	(−0.22)	(0.50)	(3.64)	(0.20)
Acres improved	−0.305	−0.486	2.593*	1.771	2.112*	2.914
	(−0.60)	(−0.82)	(3.48)	(0.52)	(3.26)	(1.56)
Stock value	0.202*	0.179	−0.202	0.333	0.074	0.102
	(3.02)	(0.175)	(−0.254)	(0.75)	(0.91)	(1.02)
Implement value	0.099	−0.306	0.625*	0.252	0.083	0.325
	(0.48)	(−1.35)	(2.79)	(0.27)	(1.18)	(1.58)
Constant	129.60*	−102.91*	−14.66*	201.61*	−161.19*	27.63*
	(2.49)	(−1.80)	(−1.74)	(1.49)	(−2.61)	(1.46)
R^2	.50	.47	.54	.07	.61	.77

Note: b-values are presented; t-values are indicated in parentheses.
*Significant at the .05 level.

cially in stable and dynamic communities), this was due to characteristics other than their residential stability.

This finding underscores the important role of migration in the agriculture transition. It demonstrates that at the individual level simply being a persister was no guarantee of greater agricultural output and that aggressive migrant farmers were quite often able to successfully compete within market regions. For example, we might have expected persisters to have done better in terms of net production than their migrating neighbors, but they did not. Migration, then, was a vehicle that reallocated human capital for greater agricultural output and economic efficiency. Very simply, commercially oriented farmers moved to areas of emerging market opportunities and left those where opportunities were not as great. On the other hand, farmers not producing a surplus product tended to remain in, or sometimes move to, marginal commercial areas of the state.

These analyses also show that a farmer's age typically had no significant relationship to net yields during the decade although the negative b-values demonstrate that younger farmers did produce slightly more (though not significantly more) than others. The one exception was in dynamic ecologies along the Erie Canal, where younger farmers had significantly greater outputs. Once again, this indicates that many younger, migratory farmers often were as productive as older, more experienced persisting farmers, especially in areas of growing economic opportunity.

While persistence and age were not significantly related to net production, agricultural inputs (acres plowed, acres improved, investment in agricultural implements, and the allocation of land to meadow) had a mixed relationship to overall net yields within ecologies. First, these analyses indicate that improving the land by itself made little difference in terms of net yields once we control for other factors. The two exceptions were dynamic ecologies in 1855 and marginal communities in 1865. However, the cultivation of land did have an effect. As might be expected, a farm household willing to invest the time and energy to plow more land (irrespective of the size of their farm) typically would have greater yields. Even as the general cultivation of field crops declined during the decade, this relationship remained significant in each market ecology.

To illustrate this point, I selected an enclave of ten successful farms from Argyle Township, Washington County. Each of these farming households was involved in the market economy and each increased their agricultural output between 1855 and 1865. Of the ten farms, seven increased their acreage under cultivation, one stayed the same, and two decreased slightly the number of acres devoted to field crops. In the latter two cases, however, the households of John Hopkins and John Moore shifted their production to dairying. The others in the enclave increased their acreage under the plow from about two to eight acres during the decade. For example, the James Hannas increased theirs from eleven to fifteen acres; the Hugh Kings, eighteen to twenty acres; the Joseph Pattersons, thirty-five to forty acres; and the William Lindsays, fourteen to sixteen acres. Although these increases were not dramatic, they represent substantially more work for these households and in each case resulted in significantly greater agricultural output.[18]

As noted in Chapter 5, investment in agricultural implements typically was not as critical as expected in determining net yields during this period. Although these investments were related to slightly higher production in dynamic ecologies in 1855, they had no significant relationship to net production in stable or marginal market areas that year. Moreover, by 1865 the relationship between tool investment and net yields had completely disappeared everywhere in the state.

There are a number of possible explanations for this. First, it appears that since nominal investments in basic agricultural implements (such as plows) had become so commonplace by 1865, they no longer effectively distinguished between levels of production. By then, most farmers owned some tools. Second, as will be discussed in Chapter 7, surplus market farm households often used their productive human capital in the form of coresident migrant working kin and boarders to supplement their capital investments and generate an agricultural surplus. Human capital investments therefore were often more important than tools. And third, New York's shift toward dairying and sheep raising during this decade made agricultural tools less critical to overall net yields than in more specialized grain-producing regions of the country such as the Midwest. Once again, in dairying and sheep raising operations, human capital was more important than the purchase of new tools or machines.

The growing importance of dairying can clearly be seen in marginal ecologies of the state. In both 1855 and 1865 the allocation of land to meadow in these areas was a significant factor in predicting net yields. These communities typically were more remote from markets. As a result some surplus-oriented farmers moved vigorously into these kinds of production throughout the decade, eventually making a big difference in their net yields.

In both stable and dynamic ecologies, on the other hand, dairying and sheep raising were so important that most farmers had begun to shift their production away from field crops to dairying and sheep raising. As a result, the allocation of land to meadow did not distinguish between their net yields.

FARM VALUE AND OUTPUT

The relationship between farm value and net agricultural output within each market ecology provides a number of insights into the fundamental changes in the rural economy during these years. In dynamic

and stable market areas, for example, the relationship between the
value of the farm and net agricultural production changed dramatically
(Table 6.4). In 1855 total farm value was related to net output only in
marginal ecologies. By the end of the decade, however, it had become
a powerful and statistically significant predictor of net production
everywhere in the state.

This demonstrates that these New Yorkers were experiencing
some basic changes during this agricultural transition. These changes
involved a shift from relative wealth homogeneity within areas where
an individual's farm value was not necessarily associated with net production, to a more stratified agricultural economy where greater farm
values and higher net yields went hand in hand. This idea is illustrated
in Table 6.5. It shows that in dynamic market ecologies the level of
stratification, as measured by the proportion of total farm value held by
the wealthiest 10 percent of the sample, grew by about 2 percent during the decade. In stable market ecologies, on the other hand, this increase was nearly 10 percent. And as expected, in marginal market areas, farm values were stratified in 1855 and declined only slightly by
the end of the Civil War as more commercial opportunities for small-
scale producers began to emerge.

A CHRONICLE OF THE AGRICULTURAL TRANSITION

Hidden within these complex relationships is a chronicle of the
mid-nineteenth-century agricultural transition. However, the transition
was neither universal nor linear but varied across time and space. Farm
families located in marginal market ecologies (typically along the Allegheny Plateau and rugged Adirondacks) of New York State were witnessing the first signs of commercial development during this decade as
a number of growing towns had begun to provide markets for a variety
of agricultural commodities. However, most of these farmers had little
experience with the surplus market economy and as a result became
only marginally associated with the marketplace. A few commercially
oriented farmers in these communities dominated the market activity
that existed, and as a result there was significant stratification of farm
values at the beginning of this decade (Table 6.5). However, as market

TABLE 6.5
Farm Values, Stratification, and Market Ecologies for 1855 and 1865

Market ecology	1855	1865
Stable		
Average farm value	$3117	$4065
Median farm value	$2750	$3500
Percentage held by the		
wealthiest 10 percent	26.2	36.1
	N = 326	N = 318
Marginal		
Average farm value	$2319	$2646
Median farm value	$1200	$1800
Percentage held by the		
wealthiest 10 percent	38.9	37.8
	N = 214	N = 151
Dynamic		
Average farm value	$3121	$4329
Median farm value	$2400	$3660
Percentage held by the		
wealthiest 10 percent	29.7	31.2
	N = 237	N = 272

opportunities grew, more farmers entered surplus market production and so there was a slight ebbing of that stratification by 1865.

Yet these communities were beginning to change, evidenced in part by their unique pattern of heavy in- and out-migration. In this mobile environment, poor but aspiring market farmers often moved a few miles to take advantage of new emerging markets or more fertile land. If successful, they might sell their farm for a small profit and move to the next township or perhaps across the county line in search of even better land or greater access to markets. Whatever its form, this short-range but furious pace of migration characterized these marginal market ecologies and appears to be typical of an early stage of the surplus market economy.[19]

Dynamic market communities, on the other hand, were dominated by slightly wealthier and significantly larger-scale producers. These commercial farm families typically supplied local markets by wagon and larger urban centers in the East by canal and rail.

There was a moderate increase in wealth stratification in these communities during the decade, partly because of the large-scale in-migration of very aggressive surplus market producers. These farm households typically migrated to dynamic communities and then remained. As a result of their unique migration profiles (high in- and low out-migration), many of these communities, with sparse populations at the turn of the nineteenth century, experienced unprecedented rates of population growth and were transformed in just twenty or thirty years. Clearly, many farmers in these communities had a strong commitment to surplus commercial activity and by the end of the decade had achieved significant levels of agricultural production.

Finally, in stable market ecologies, most farmers were producing for market by 1865, and their net production was impressive. Communities of this sort had a long history of market involvement in the river trade along the Hudson and later by canal and rail feeders. As a result, by 1865 the yeoman farmer producing below surplus, still numerous in other parts of the state, had all but disappeared in these areas.

Some of these yeoman farmers had made the transition to surplus market production; others had out-migrated to areas with cheaper land; and still others moved to cities where they may have tried their hand at nonagricultural work. But much of this migration activity had occurred before 1855 because by that date these areas were the most stable in the state, with relatively lower levels of both in-migration and out-migration.

Recognizing their strong market position, farmers in stable ecologies typically transferred their land to their sons, who in turn often remained in the community for their entire life. As a result of these factors, stable market ecologies had become quite stratified by 1865. Located in the richest, most commercially active areas of the state, these farmers were the archetypical large-scale producers of their day, whose competitive power had grown to the point that they had begun to successfully "squeeze out" both the yeoman and the small-scale commercial producer.

Thus, by examining the level of surplus market development in the context of emerging market ecologies, we can begin to appreciate the complexity of the agricultural transition in the middle decades of the nineteenth century. Moreover, we are able to understand more fully the role of New York's culture of mobility in facilitating this fundamental transformation of the agricultural economy and society.

Migrating kith and kin could help the farm family reap the elusive surplus from their acres.

Family Structure
as a Market Strategy

B y 1865 surplus market farmers throughout upstate New York had strengthened their economic position by capitalizing on new market opportunities, especially those that had emerged as a result of the Civil War. Farmers used their land more intensively, sometimes by increasing their field crops but more often by converting unimproved acreage into pasture or meadow to support sheep raising and dairying. Most upgraded their agricultural tool inventories. Also, many of these farmers used migration as a vehicle to help them produce a surplus for market.

Yet this was only part of the story. Beyond their internal migration, new production strategies, and capital investments, New York farmers often increased their yields by maximizing the human capital of their households. These farm families understood that the development of their household resources was essential for successful surplus market involvement. Moreover, by increasing their production within the context of their households, these farmers could achieve their economic goals and maintain their traditional kin relations and production patterns.

Many mid-nineteenth-century farmers recognized that their extensive labor needs were not well served by young children who might be eager to help but were not always capable of the grueling work necessary for surplus market production. Some farmers, of course, hired farm laborers to work for a month or an entire season. But as the wages of farm laborers rose, these costs became prohibitive. As a result, some farmers began to turn to a new source of adult farm labor to satisfy their growing labor requirements: their migrating kin.

These farm families often extended their households with migrant relatives who could contribute to their production for a time before they moved on in search of their own financial independence in the next township, across the county line, or in another state. In return for their labor, these migrant relatives received training, lodging, information about the area, and perhaps financial and emotional support. Surplus market farmers of all ages used this strategy of household extension, but it was most common among those in their late twenties and early thirties who typically had fewer older productive children in the household.

However, these kinds of household extension strategies have received little scholarly attention. As noted, the identification of surplus market farm households in the past has been a difficult theoretical and empirical exercise. And although historians have become increasingly sensitive to the importance of internal migration, most studies focus exclusively on the movement of household heads, and as a result, they provide few insights into the migration of other family members.[1] Because of these problems most scholarship on the changing structure of rural households has not considered fully the role of migration nor its relationship to agricultural change.

PROGRESSIVE NUCLEATION

The most enduring general model of household change has been "progressive nucleation." Developed primarily by sociologists such as Louis Wirth, Talcott Parsons, and others in the 1930s, 1940s, and 1950s, this model reflected the conventional popular wisdom about the perceived crisis of the family. These scholars typically argued that traditional households had been extended with loving relatives providing support and domestic warmth for one another. These strong social moorings were the cohesive bonds upon which the gemeinschaft of traditional society was built. But with the coming of industrialization, these intimate bonds were broken, and the result was the emergence of the sterile, anomic, nuclear household.[2]

This theory slowly was abandoned in the 1960s when Peter Laslett and his colleagues of the Cambridge group demonstrated that neither the extended nor the stem household had ever been the dominant family form. Rather, they argued that the nuclear household, the accepted hallmark of modern society, had been the typical Western family type since at least 1599.[3]

But in the process of rejecting the theory of progressive nucleation, scholars developed few, if any, alternative hypotheses that could fully explain variations in household structure. In fact, a number of scholars argued that Western households had always been nuclear, creating what Edward Shorter once called the fantasy of "nuclear family as historical constant."[4]

Some scholars challenged this assumption, noting a close connection between the life course and household organization. In the early 1970s, for example, Tamara Hareven showed that the household was not a static entity but a "process" in constant demographic change. Lutz Berkner also demonstrated that the developmental cycle of the family often dictated the structure of households in the past. He argued that the scarcity of stem families among the peasantry in eighteenth-century Austria had resulted from demographic constraints to their formation such as early mortality and late marriage of family members. More recently, Steven Ruggles used a micro simulation model to determine the "propensities" of family members to coreside with their kin over time. He noted that "a great deal of variation in family structure is a product of variation in demographic conditions." Finally, Michael Anderson showed that families often were extended in the past since "kin provided the [primary] source of ... nurture in old age or sickness which [was] not available from any other source."[5]

Thus our understanding of changes in household structure was not complete. Clearly, the ubiquitous nuclear household was as much a historical fantasy as progressive nucleation had proved to be. And while two decades of family research had demonstrated that there were critical variations in the structure of households in the past, beyond those associated with the nurture of older or sick family members, there appeared to be no pattern or meaning to it. Was the household structured exclusively by the life course, or did economic change such as the emergence of the commercial agricultural economy also have an effect? The present research on mid-nineteenth-century farm households demonstrates that there was a strong association between changes in the economic environment and alterations in the structure of the household, with migration acting as an important catalyst.

LIFE-COURSE NURTURE EXTENSIONS

As in other communities throughout history, New York farmers typically used the family to provide support for the aged and infirm. As household members aged, their familial roles changed in a seemingly endless cycle. The inexorable and well-known passage of a man from son to apprentice farmer to household head and father to aging patriarch was repeated thousands of times. The growth and maturation of a young woman from daughter to wife, mother, and then learned grandmother was also a natural part of the life course. And while the loss of a mate would temporarily alter the basic structure of the household, this too was a familiar part of life.

Young adult rural New Yorkers tended to cling to their families, with nearly one in five living with their parents or other relative. As they aged, some left home to begin their own families. From this point through late middle age, farm families typically were nuclear, with only about a fifth to a quarter living with relatives. However, when New York household heads reached their mid-fifties, they were once again more likely to be found living with their relatives, with nearly half having at least one coresident kin in their homes. This general cycle was typical of all New Yorkers, although it varied somewhat by ethnicity and, as we will see, involvement in the surplus market economy. One of the primary reasons for life-course nurture extension among mid-century New Yorkers was the care and succor of a parent, especially older widows. About four in ten New Yorkers older than fifty-five (44.4 percent) were found living in an extended household in 1855, but nearly 60 percent of these retained their status as household heads, with kin forming a subfamily in their home. But with the loss of a mate, things changed dramatically. Among those older New Yorkers who had lost either a husband or wife, only one in three retained their status as head of household, with two of three moving in with their middle-aged children. Thus, it was not the onset of old age alone but the combination of advanced years, sickness, and the loss of a mate that usually signaled both the end of household head status and the formation of the extended household.

A comparison of the widow Rachel Wright from Farmersville and George and Mary Giles of Argyle, New York, illustrates this point. Rachel, age fifty-five, recently had lost her husband and probably as a result had become the dependent member of her son Orin's household. The Gileses, on the other hand, were about the same age as Rachel but were still firmly in control of a large extended household. George, age fifty-six, was a yeoman farmer living in a modest frame home with Mary, their four children, and George's elderly mother-in-law.[6]

RECIPROCAL ECONOMIC EXTENSIONS

Life-course nurture extensions, however, were only part of the reason for changes in family structure. With the dramatic growth of new opportunities in the nineteenth century, triggered by economic change, an increasing number of young, productive rural men and women sought social and economic advancement through migration. These migrants needed a place to live, some emotional support, and information to achieve their goals, and surplus market host families often met these needs in return for labor.

Figure 7.1 illustrates these relationships and identifies the hypothesized causal links between the emergence of surplus commercial agriculture, internal migration, and household change. In this model, the growth of surplus market opportunities in the rural economy (and changes in material tastes) triggered in- and out-migration. Because migration was played out in the context of the household, the family also changed.

This model is based on two assumptions. The first is that the volume of migration in a community varied directly with economic change; the second is that migration typically operated in the context of

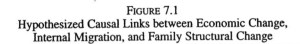

FIGURE 7.1
Hypothesized Causal Links between Economic Change,
Internal Migration, and Family Structural Change

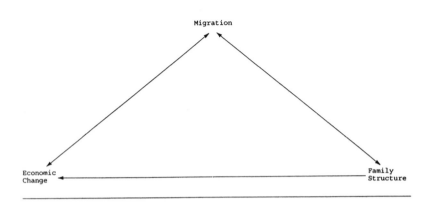

the household. The first assumption has been an accepted tenant of migration research since E.G. Ravenstein published his classic theories more than a century ago. The basic premise here is that young, productive men and women often migrated for economic reasons: they were either "pushed" from their communities of origin or "pulled" to new ones. Although the general "gravity" model of migration and immigration has been modified in recent years, most scholars would agree that changes in the structure or activity of the economy often are associated with some form of migration.[7]

Research on internal migration in the last several decades has demonstrated that economic change and migration are strongly associated, and at the same time, scholars have shown that internal migration typically was a family affair and less often an isolated, solitary activity. As discussed in Chapter 2, the family was central to the migration pageant. Even the lone migrant often depended on information and housing provided by kin networks and family support in the sending and receiving communities.[8]

In short, numerous scholars have demonstrated that the process of migration was important in expanding the role and structural complexity of the household. The needs of family members moving from one community (urban or rural) to another (often as a result of changing economic opportunities) typically were met by relatives at the end of the journey. Families provided migrants with information and housing in the new community, and they offered financial assistance and emotional support for the newcomer. In return, migrants provided a valuable labor service for the host family.

Jonah Ransom of Greene County, introduced in Chapter 5, illustrates this form of extension. In 1855 Jonah lived with his wife and children in a nuclear family and scratched out a living as a yeoman farmer. However, sometime after 1855 the Ransoms brought three young relatives into their household to assist them with farm production. By 1865 they apparently had achieved their goal and were firmly part of the surplus market economy of the county.[9]

Structural changes in the household, therefore, were directly related to economic change and mediated by the process of migration. In agricultural (or industrial) economies with relatively few new opportunities for employment or surplus market involvement, there would be less internal migration, and therefore we would expect that most households would be nuclear—and they were.

In the relatively stable agrarian-based economy of Laslett's seventeenth-century England, for example, fewer people were on the move, relative to the nineteenth century, and as a result there were fewer extended households (about 10 percent at the cross-sectional level). As expected, most of these extensions were related to family nurture during the life course.

However, with the emergence of the surplus market economy and industrialization in the nineteenth century, there was a dramatic rise in the volume of migration (see Chapter 2) and an associated increase in the level of extended household formation (see Figure 7.2). Although some of this was due to changes in the demography of households, such as an increase in life expectancy, it seems clear that reciprocal economic extensions related to migration also played a part.

SURPLUS MARKET HOUSEHOLDS

The migration of younger, productive migrants through farm households at mid-nineteenth century allowed aspiring surplus market farmers to use available household resources and exploit emerging

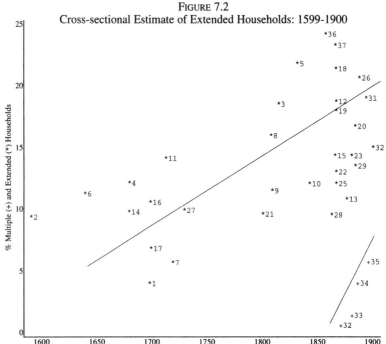

FIGURE 7.2
Cross-sectional Estimate of Extended Households: 1599-1900

Data were derived from the following sources (see bibliography): 1-31, Laslett, "Characteristics of the Western Family," Table 1.1; 32-35, Seward, Household versus Family Membership"; 36, from Parkerson, "The People of New York "State"; and 37, Anderson, "Family Structure," Table 8,44.

commercial opportunities. As a result of these reciprocal economic extensions, market producers were much more likely than yeoman to be living with or near their relatives (see Table 7.1). These differences can be seen in a number of ways. First, while more than one in four surplus farmers lived in extended households in 1855, fewer than one in five yeoman did likewise. Second, market farmers were more likely to have *working* male relatives living in their households (24.3 versus 15.8 percent). And finally, these farmers were significantly more likely than yeomen to be living within five households of their kin (22.7 versus 18.3 percent).[10] It also should be noted that surplus market farmers were significantly more likely to have co-resident boarders (relatives or strangers) than their yeomen neighbors in both 1855 and 1865.

Yeoman farmers did have slightly larger households in 1855 (significant in 1865), but this was because they typically had more chil-

TABLE 7.1
Household Structure for 1855 and 1865
(Percent in each category unless noted)

Family type	All farmers		Yeomen		Surplus market farmers	
	1855	1865	1855	1865	1855	1865
Extended household	23.0	22.2	19.8	18.2	25.6	23.9
Relatives nearby[a]	20.7	21.1	18.3	18.2	22.7	22.6
Male boarders	6.6	3.7	4.8	3.5	7.9	3.8
Female boarders	2.9	2.1	2.0	1.7	3.2	2.3
Male kin with occupation	23.2	25.2	15.8	23.5	24.3	26.0
Female kin with occupation	3.7	2.2	4.8	2.2^n	2.7	2.2^n
People in household (number)	5.4	5.3	5.5^n	5.8	5.4^n	5.1
Adults in household (number)[n]	2.9	2.9	2.8	2.9	3.1	3.0
Percent adults in household	54.7	54.1	50.9	50.0	59.2	58.8
Children in household (number)	2.5	2.4	2.5^n	2.9	2.2^n	2.1
Children ever born (number)[b]	—	4.5	—	4.9	—	4.3
	N = 777	N = 738	N = 348	N = 225	N = 429	N = 513

Note: All differences between yeomen and surplus market farmers are significant at the .05 level in both 1855 and 1865 unless noted.
    [a]This measure was determined by searching for same-surname relatives within five dwellings on either side of the sample individual. It should be noted that this figure is a lower bound estimate because it does not include the relatives of the spouse.
    [b]The 1865 New York State Census asked the number of children ever born to the spouse of the head. This data was not included in the 1855 census.
    [n]Differences that are not significant.

dren. Surplus market families usually had fewer children in the home and more often had productive older males and females in their households.

By 1865 little had changed in this regard. In fact, most of the differences in household structure between surplus market farmers and yeoman remained statistically significant by the end of the Civil War, although there were some changes in the overall totals by that date. Surplus market farmers were still more likely to have co-resident kin and unrelated adult male and female boarders in their household. In fact, there was a significant difference in the proportion of adults in the households of each of these groups. In both 1855 and 1865 surplus market households were about 60 percent adult, whereas yeoman households were about 50 percent adult. In short, the surplus market farmer and not the more traditional yeoman was more likely to maintain an extended household, live in close proximity to relatives, and have unrelated boarders and working kin in the household as well as a larger adult population. Partly as a result of these strategies, it can be argued, surplus market households had much greater farm and per-acre yields.

CHILDREN AND AGRICULTURAL PRODUCTION

An important question remains. Why didn't aspiring surplus market farmers simply use their children as laborers rather than boarding their kith and kin to maximize production? The conventional wisdom, of course, has always been that a large brood of children was one of the foremost signs of a prosperous farmer. However, as we know, conventional "wisdom" is not necessarily wise. Indeed, an examination of the census manuscripts reveals that farm boys in upstate New York rarely were listed as farmers or as having any occupation, for that matter, before about age fifteen. This suggests the generally low utility assigned to young farm children.

Recently, Lee Craig has demonstrated empirically that young farm children were not very productive. Craig reanalyzed the "Bateman-Foust sample" of northern rural households in 1860 and demonstrated that children in their pre-teen years did not add significantly to the production of the family farm. In fact, their presence in a household significantly *lowered* farm production. On the other hand, he found that older children, especially teenage boys, did make a significant contribution to a family's agricultural production even when other factors were taken into account. I have replicated these findings for mid-nineteenth-century New York State.[11] Of course, young children could be useful on the family farm, doing whatever they could to help out. But they could not strip hemlock bark, chop cords of wood, haul charcoal from deep in the forest, cut and stack sheaves of wheat, or participate in many of the other strenuous farm activities that we have seen helped thousands of New York farm families to survive or enter the surplus market economy.

Moreover, when children reached physical maturity, there certainly was no guarantee that they would not leave the household to seek their fortunes elsewhere. Recently, David Galenson demonstrated that the average age for sons to leave home during the nineteenth century was eighteen years old and that by age twenty-one, 80 percent had departed. Although he notes that sons in agricultural homes left slightly later, his figures show that most farm sons did not remain at home for long once they had matured physically.[12]

Thus it appears that while younger children could be helpful on the family farm, many farmers recognized that their productive utility was limited to just a few years between the onset of physical maturity and their departure from the homestead. Clearly, raising "a brood" of children so that they might eventually help out on the family farm was a poor investment strategy.

MIGRATING WORKERS

While older children might be productive on the family farm for a brief time in the life cycle, adult in-migrant men and women had immediate greater potential as workers. When these migrant kin or strangers moved on, perhaps to buy their own farm or to marry, they could be replaced if necessary by other adult migrants. In short, by relying on adult workers (often migrant kin and sometimes strangers) rather than young children, surplus market farm families could improve their yields immediately by enhancing the human capital of their household.

Numerous examples of this strategy can be found in the census manuscripts, and the weight of the quantitative evidence is compelling. For example, while overall differences in household organization between surplus market and yeoman farmers are evident at all ages (i.e., the former were more likely to live with their kin), when we examine each cohort separately, these differentials become even more dramatic.

Table 7.2 shows the percentage of New York farmers in 1855 and 1865 living in extended households by age cohort and surplus production. Among young marrieds, age twenty-five to thirty-five in 1855, about a third (32.4 percent) of the surplus farm households were extended, whereas less than one in four yeomen families had coresident relatives. In 1865 nearly four in ten (38.5 percent) of the former group

TABLE 7.2
Percentage Living in Extended Households by Age Group

Stage in life cycle	1855	N	1865	N
Young people (15-24 years)[a]	29.5	44	—	—
Yeomen	16.1	31	—	—
Surplus market	46.2	13	—	—
Young marrieds (25-34 years)	28.0	193	34.8	92
Yeomen	23.9	88	25.9	27
Surplus market	32.4	105	38.5	65
Maturing families (35-44 years)	21.2	189	20.6	189
Yeomen	19.1	89	19.0	63
Surplus market	23.4	107	21.4	126
Completed families (45-54 years)	20.1	189	15.0	220
Yeomen	16.5	79	8.2	73
Surplus market	22.7	110	19.0	147
Seniors (55 years and older)	22.8	162	22.7	216
Yeomen	17.1	70	20.8	53
Surplus market	27.2	92	23.3	163

[a]Young people were not included in the 1865 data because there were too few cases.

lived with their relatives, and only a quarter (25.9 percent) of young married yeomen did likewise. Given the discussion above, this pattern was expected. These farmers presumably had young children in their households (younger than age fifteen) if they had children at all and may have lacked the human capital necessary to produce a surplus. As a result, it appears that they often extended their households with migrant working kin to help them with their farmwork. However, we have seen that yeomen did not adopt these strategies as often.

As these surplus market household heads matured (age thirty-five to forty-four), many of them presumably would have had children capable of sustained farmwork. These children, roughly between the ages of fifteen and twenty-five, could be productive if they remained on the farm, and using Galenson's figures we can estimate that about one in five would do so after the age of twenty-one.[13] With these more productive workers, surplus market farm households apparently did not find it necessary as often to bring other migrating adult relatives into their homes. Consequently, we can see a sharp decline in the level of household extensions (32.4 to 23.4 percent in 1855 and 38.5 to 21.4 percent in 1865).

These findings are suggestive of the household strategies families used during this period to maximize their human capital and thereby help them produce a surplus for market. In Chapter 4 we saw that surplus market farmers used their land more intensively and upgraded their agricultural implement inventories more often than yeomen. Thus, plowing more land for field crops, converting land into meadow or pasture, and making nominal capital investments in tools were important strategies for successful surplus market involvement. But these alone cannot explain fully the dramatic differences we find in net production. Clearly, there was a critical human capital component to be considered here, revealed in both the structure and corresponding net agricultural output of surplus market households.

One final note is in order. It could be argued that wealthier surplus market households would be more likely to be extended simply because they had the financial resources to support other family members. This argument seems logical, but it can be rejected for several reasons. First, the literature on household extension discussed above demonstrates that very poor people often brought relatives into their homes. William Ross, Sr., mentioned in Chapter 2, is a good example. William had settled in New York in 1848 and seven years later was still a glove cutter in a local factory. He lived in a cramped cabin valued at less than one hundred dollars but nevertheless supported two in-laws as well as his own large family and provided some support for his son Thomas when he migrated to the community in early 1855. These and many other examples suggest that the wealthy had no monopoly on assisting their kin through co-residence. In other words, *both* surplus market farmers and yeoman households provided nurture for poor relatives, older in-laws, orphans, etc. The difference, as discussed above, was that surplus market families more often extended their households with lateral working kin (uncles, cousins, nephews) as well.

Second, if wealth was the primary factor that determined household organization, we would expect an increase in household extension as the head of the household aged and presumably achieved a stronger economic position. This was not the case, although as expected, there was a slight increase in nurture extensions among seniors. More importantly, we have seen that lateral and upward extensions of surplus market farm households were most common in the early married years of farm families when their children were very young and their economic position was more tenuous. Extensions then declined sharply after age thirty-five, at the very time when the family presumably was in a stronger economic position.

Third, we might expect to find fewer working kin in wealthier surplus market households if nurture was the exclusive function of extension. Once again, however, this was not the case. These farm households had a significantly greater percentage of working kin in their families, which suggests that they played an important productive function rather than simply a dependent one.

Finally, there are numerous examples in this sample in which we can actually see the link between household extension with productive migrant relatives and a movement from yeoman to surplus market production. The case of the Jonah Ransom family is one of them. The Ransoms were yeoman farmers in 1855, but in the decade that followed they brought three young male relatives into their household who apparently helped improve their agricultural yield and produce a substantial surplus by 1865. This movement into the surplus market economy was achieved without any additional investments in agricultural tools.

Although it is difficult to impute causality using these data, the weight of this evidence, both quantitative and qualitative, is compelling. Surplus market households clearly extended their families to help destitute relatives, but they also brought younger, productive migrant workers into the household to help increase net yields.

By extending their households with migrant working kin, especially when their children were very young and unable to contribute significantly to the household workforce, surplus market farm families in mid-nineteenth-century New York were able to control more carefully their economic destinies. With only modest capital investments they could clear and improve more land, provide more intensive cultivation and care for their field crops, and nurture more farm animals. In short, they could more effectively use their household resources to help them either enter or maintain their position in the surplus market economy and consumer culture.

Migrants and host families had specific needs that could be satisfied only through kin cooperation and coresidence. Migrants needed emotional support, a place to live, and knowledge of the emerging marketplace. Host families, especially in their early married years, needed willing workers who could improve their human capital and help them enter the market economy. But as Anderson notes, "When it became possible for actors to maximize satisfaction without recourse to kin, kin obligations were indeed rejected."[14]

Apparently this is exactly what many mid-nineteenth-century New York farmers did. As their young children reached physical maturity in their teen years, the family was able to abandon migrant kin as household workers. As a result, the need to extend the family declined rapidly, and the percentage of extended households dropped. But even as these economic needs for extensions disappeared, life-course nurture extensions persisted, with widows, orphans, and penniless relatives continuing to move in with their families whether they were part of the surplus market economy or not.

"The farmer pays for all" (ca. 1869).

Migration and the
Agricultural Transition

By the summer of 1865 farm families like the Jonah Ransoms, the Benjamin Gues, and the Porter Blisses could look back on the previous decades with a mixture of pride and anguish. Each had struggled to enter the surplus market economy, and each had achieved a measure of success against the backdrop of an American tragedy. The horrors of the Civil War were still vivid in the minds of these men and women, and though the events at Appomattox Courthouse had caused a measure of relief, the death of their beloved President Lincoln had cast a dark shadow over it.

Yet life would go on. Despite the sorrow and confusion of the day, the summer of 1865 was a time of continued optimism for many mid-nineteenth-century New Yorkers. The crops would be ready for harvest in a month or two, and soon growing sons and daughters would take their place in ebullient postwar New York. Men and women like the Ransoms, Gues, and Blisses were part of a fortunate generation of farmers. Born in the first decades of the nineteenth century, they had seen their small nation grow dramatically and its economy prosper beyond their most fantastic dreams.

The farmers of this generation had within them a curious mixture of individual self-interest and respect for the strong bonds of family and kinship. Some rejected the emerging commercial economy altogether. Others eagerly awaited the construction of canals and railroads and the development of new technologies to help them transform their agricultural production from semi-subsistence to surplus market production. Still others were attracted to material consumerism and slowly abandoned the rustic, though often dreary, simplicity of yeomanry for a piece of the "good life." But whether these farmers shunned the market, entered it directly as businesspeople, or more indirectly as consumers, few recognized that the purchase of a power loom carpet, a few yards of cloth, a new farm wagon or steel face plow would set in motion a process that would alter fundamentally their lives and the lives of their children and grandchildren.

The agricultural transition of New York during the middle of the nineteenth century was partly the story of the rise of an emerging class of surplus market farmers and partly a tale of a more subtle process involving the rise of the consumer society that embraced *both* materialism and the traditional values associated with kinship and family. We should remember that it was the farm families of the mid-nineteenth century who nurtured the growth of industrialization by purchasing the inexpensive and sometimes crudely fashioned goods that were produced in factories and sweatshops. In an era when most Americans still lived in rural or farming communities, it also follows that many of the consumers of factory goods, produced by a very small industrial proletariat, were rural, often farming, people.

The linchpin of the agricultural transition was this generation's unique culture of mobility, which not only nurtured the development of the surplus market economy but also made urbanization and industrialization possible. Without the voluntary migration of thousands of farmers to agricultural communities that offered new opportunities as well as to the cities themselves, this economic transition could not have occurred.

The onset of this culture of mobility was dramatic and unexpected. In the second quarter of the nineteenth century, we can document a significant increase in internal migration. For example, net migration rates more than doubled during the first half of the nineteenth century, and estimates of out-migration (derived from the historical persistence literature) also increased significantly. By mid-nineteenth century, the typical community studied by historians and economists experienced an unprecedented out-migration rate of more than 60 percent! This furious pace of internal migration continued throughout the nineteenth century, although it slowed somewhat by the middle of the twentieth century.[1]

However, as we have seen, persistent historiographical traditions and problems of measurement have made it difficult for us to understand fully the role of migration in the past. Early interpretations of American economic and social development typically overlooked ordinary men *and* women, and as a result, the migration of millions of Americans received only limited attention. Although "new social historians" have effectively refocused our attention on the common folk in the last several decades, they too have had some difficulty in interpreting population mobility. Here, the primary problems are methodological.[2]

But if our understanding of the *general* process of migration is limited, then our perspective on rural population movement is hidden behind an even darker veil of mystery. As we have seen, the persistent image of nineteenth-century rural America typically has been bucolic and pastoral, contrasting sharply with the bustling, mobile city. However, these stereotypes represent an egregious misunderstanding of migration during this time.

Although hundreds of contemporary observers of nineteenth-century America, including the incomparable Alexis de Tocqueville, noted a remarkable turnover of population in the countryside, the pastoral image of an immobile rural population has persisted. Ironically, part of the problem here is the rather negative, if not pathological, stereotype of transient cities. Indeed, the image of an uprooted, anomic, and transient urban society wrenched from the gemeinschaft of traditional family and community ties often found a convenient counterpoint in a static, staid, and sleepy countryside. This image was very simple: City people moved a great deal, and country folk remained rooted in their communities.

The other major component of this misconception is methodological. In their attempt to measure accurately residential persistence in communities during the nineteenth century, historians have used the technique of nominal record linkage. While extremely valuable, this technique suffers the limitations of measuring a residual. Simply put, the persistence rate (which results from nominal record linkage) is the percentage of people identified on a population list who can be traced to another list a decade later. Those not found are presumed to be out-migrants. But people might also be missing from the second list because of mortality, census enumerator omission, and the problem of ethnic common names. And since mortality, underenumeration, and ethnic common names were much more prevalent in nineteenth-century cities, urban places typically have been seen as more transient, thus further reinforcing the traditional stereotype.

Therefore, the apparent transiency of nineteenth century cities vis-à-vis the countryside was partly an illusion based on both enduring historiographical traditions and methodological problems. Indeed, Tocqueville and other contemporary observers may have been right after all. The countryside was in constant motion, with rural people moving in perhaps even greater numbers than their urban cousins.

Migration, of course, did not occur in a vacuum, nor was it simply a "strange unrest," as Tocqueville once called it, isolated from the important economic changes of nineteenth-century America. In fact, we have seen that the extraordinary migration of rural Americans during this period was a central feature of the agricultural transition.

But like the process of migration itself, we have not understood the agricultural transition very well. We have seen that New York farming during this period was a strange brew of both semi-subsistence and commercial activities. And although it is clear that most farmers had at least occasional contact with the market, not all were well integrated into the surplus market economy. Nevertheless, there was a rather remarkable transition toward surplus market production during these years.

This transition was accompanied by a marked increase in the stratification of New York agricultural communities. Although landowner-ship remained widespread by the end of the Civil War, farm values had become much more differentiated. Surplus market farms increased rapidly in value, while the price of yeoman land remained static or fell. Clearly, a kind of sorting-out process had begun. Farmers in search of a surplus were very aggressive. They migrated to communities that offered market opportunities, they plowed more land, they upgraded their tools, they acquired more livestock, they carefully invested their profits, and they drew heavily on their available human resources to increase their production. Indeed, by the summer of 1865 New York State had begun its long odyssey toward a more consolidated agricultural economy in which wealth increasingly was controlled by fewer and fewer farmers with larger, more productive farms.

But how did the elusive process of migration relate to the equally elusive agriculture transition? The answer to this question is complex and involves both individual and ecological perspectives. At the individual level, we have seen that migration was both a strategy of survival and a vehicle of self-improvement. Each of these scenarios was played out in the context of the family. For the poor, the destitute, the abandoned, the widowed, the sick, the very young, and the very old, migration became a mechanism of survival to find support from family members in another town, county, state, or region.

However, many farmers also used migration as a vehicle of upward mobility and as a possible admission ticket to the surplus market economy. Many migrants began their careers without the benefit of an inheritance, but most had wealth of a different sort: family connections in both their places of origin and destination. Many migrants achieved success in the surplus commercial economy, especially if they chose the right market area as their ultimate destination. Farmers who migrated to commercial centers along the Erie Canal, for example, had net yields larger than all others in New York State, including persisting farmers who had inherited the family farm and remained in their communities throughout their lives.

Although it was difficult to achieve commercial success if one's migration journey was a long one, say, from another state or Europe, many succeeded by relying on their kin during the initial settlement period and then persisting in their new communities. These migrants did even better if they chose growth areas for their place of destination. In short, whereas migration could be risky business, it also could pay high dividends when coupled with a bit of planning, the help of relatives, some hard work, and, of course, a great deal of luck.

However, there is much more to this story. Beyond these direct, individual effects of migration was its ecological or community level impact. By mid-nineteenth century, we can see the emergence of a number of distinct market ecologies in upstate New York. These ecologies reflected a strong association between economic and historic development and internal migration measured at the ecological level.

In marginal ecologies, farmers were witnessing the first signs of commercial market activity as small villages developed into towns and demanded a variety of agricultural commodities. The shifting opportunity structure in these communities was accompanied by a great deal of short-range in- and out-migration. Only a handful of farmers had made the move to surplus production in these marginal ecologies by 1865, but they dominated most of its activity. As a result, these communities remained economically stratified throughout the decade.

Dynamic market ecologies, on the other hand, were dominated by a slightly wealthier, moderate-scale surplus market farmer. These booming communities were characterized by greater commercial opportunities resulting from regional urban growth. As a result, they attracted large numbers of aggressive in-migrants and held on to these settlers once they arrived. Unlike the population "revolving door" of marginal market areas, the metaphor of a population magnet was more appropriate for these communities. Perhaps as a result of these migration patterns, wealth stratification also was moderate. In many ways these communities represented the archetypical American Dream of individual opportunity coupled with vigorous economic growth.

Finally, stable market ecologies along New York's river valleys had relatively little migration activity, were much older historically, and had well-established patterns of market activity. Here, the yeoman had all but disappeared, replaced by a homogeneous group of successful surplus market farmers. These farmers gradually had come to dominate the best land, available markets, and overall wealth through consistent intergenerational transfer of land and residential persistence. Clearly, these communities were well on their way toward a stratified and more consolidated agricultural economy.

In short, beyond the individual act of migration was the equally important place of destination. That choice could either make or break aspiring farmers. If the farm family's timing was right, if they had sufficient capital, and if their familial connections were well developed, they had a good chance of success in both marginal and dynamic ecologies. But to migrate to older, established, stable ecologies more often than not meant that hard times were ahead.

Even under the most difficult circumstances, some farmers showed that they could be very clever. Many were able to beat the odds and enter the surplus market economy even if they were relatively poor. They could achieve a measure of success by extending their households with migrating kin. In this way, with little monetary investment, they could supplement their human capital to increase their agricultural yields and thereby improve their chances for success in the competitive world of surplus commercial agriculture.

The enormous numbers of migrating men and women of the nineteenth century constituted an integral part of New York's unique culture of mobility and provided a great deal of the raw courage, determination, and hard work necessary to produce that elusive surplus. Beyond the many inventions, agricultural journals, countless canals and railroads, and unceasing booster rhetoric of the rural editors were these nearly forgotten common folk: the restless migrating men and women who helped facilitate the agricultural transition of New York and the nation as a whole.

The millions of men and women who streamed across the rugged landscape of mid-nineteenth century and transformed New York from a frontier settlement into the Empire State have long since departed. But their legacy remains. It remains in both a powerful commercial agricultural economy and a social structure that clings to the ideals of the family and kin within the matrix of powerful individual interest.

Samples and Map

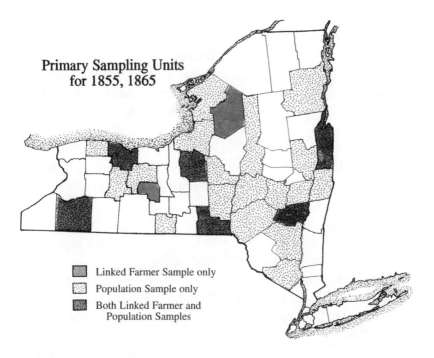

Primary Sampling Units
for 1855, 1865

- ☐ Linked Farmer Sample only
- ☐ Population Sample only
- ■ Both Linked Farmer and
  Population Samples

T he quantitative analysis in this book is based in part on two
samples. The first, the 1855 Population Sample (N ≅ 6000), is
a stratified/random sample of upstate New York in 1855 (New
York City is excluded). This sample was stratified by section of the

state (Hudson River Valley, Erie Canal corridor, northern Adirondacks, and Allegheny Plateau) and community size (urban and rural). Urban communities were oversampled, but the sample could be weighted during analysis to reflect the true urban rural population distribution at mid-nineteenth century. The sample was drawn from the population schedules of the 1855 New York State Census, with a target population of all males and females fifteen years of age or older.

The second, the "linked farmer sample" (N $\cong$ 1500), has three components: out-migrants from New York towns, 1855–65; persisters, 1855–65; and in-migrants to New York towns, 1855–65. Farmers were linked (traced forward and backward) from the 1855 New York State Census to the 1865 New York State Census and from the 1865 New York State Census to the 1855 New York State Census. Those located (forward linkage) in the two census documents were identified as "persisters," those who could not be linked from 1855 to 1865 were presumed to be "out-migrants," and those who appeared in 1865 but were not present (backward linkage) in 1855 were identified as "in-migrants."

The linked farmer sample has a target population of all producing farmers in New York State, specifically those who were listed in the agricultural schedules (either or both) of the 1855 and 1865 New York State censuses.

As with the 1855 sample, the linked farmer sample was stratified by section of the state in order to reflect the general farming population distribution of upstate New York at mid-nineteenth century.

The actual sample selection process for both samples was rather straightforward. In the 1855 sample (Population Sample), primary sampling units (PSUs) (counties, see below) were selected within each stratified section, and individuals were chosen from a randomly selected line on the population schedule. If an individual did not meet the criteria for selection (for example, if he or she was under the age of fifteen), the process was repeated until the target sample N was achieved.

The selection procedure was somewhat different and more complex for the linked farmer sample. First, PSUs (counties) were selected within each section of the state. From these, three target townships (see below) were selected randomly for each PSU. Individual farmers then were selected randomly to conform to a target N for that PSU (i.e., to reflect the agricultural population of that section). Each farmer then was hand linked to the population schedule.

Once the "core" sample from 1855 had been selected, farmers were forward linked to the same town in the 1865 agricultural schedules. To accomplish this, farmers in the target 1865 agricultural schedule were listed with their full names, page, and line numbers. These names then were alphabetized to facilitate linkage. Positive links were identified as persisters, and those missing from the second schedule were considered to be out-migrants. The mortality schedules were searched for possible decedents (thought to be out-migrants), but mortality continues to be a problem here as it is in all linkage studies.

The identification of in-migrants to 1865 was accomplished through a backward linkage. All farmers in the target 1855 agricultural schedules were listed and alphabetized as above. Farmers present in the 1865 document but not in the 1855 document were presumed to be in-migrants.

It should be noted that persistence and migration are defined narrowly. If an individual moved from one town to another and therefore was not listed in both documents in the schedules of that same town, the individual was considered to be a migrant (either out- or in-). Thus, any intertown move was considered to be a migration.

One important note is in order here. The linked farmer sample was drawn from the agricultural schedules of the 1855 and 1865 New York State censuses. As a result the actual "target population" of this study was all farmers (owners and tenants) who produced any agricultural product, including field crops, milk, butter, apples, wool, etc. Only kitchen garden products were not considered agricultural production. Since one of the primary purposes of this study was to examine agricultural production, this sampling strategy was acceptable.

However, this population did not reflect all farmers in New York State because it did not include individuals who were listed as farmers but who did not directly produce a crop. These individuals include farm laborers who had independent households and worked for other farmers as well as farm laborers who were members of producing farm households as borders or relatives. These farmers clearly were involved in farming but were what Allan Bogue has called "farmers without farms."[1]

A few examples will help clarify the actual nature of the farming population of New York in the middle of the nineteenth century. According to the published census of 1855, there were 321,930 farmers listed in the population schedules but only 231,740 returns on the agricultural census. Thus, 71.9 percent of all farmers produced an agricultural product, and 28.1 percent of all farmers were presumably "farm laborers." These figures compare to Bogue's estimates of farmers without farms in three midwestern townships in 1850 and 1860 that range from 4.1 to 32.6 percent.[2]

I also estimated that of the producing farmers of 1855 (those listed in both the population and agricultural schedules), 89.1 percent owned land whereas 10.9 percent did not. On the other hand, among all farmers (those listing "farmer" as their occupation in the population schedules), only 79.2 percent owned land and 19.8 percent did not. In short, it appears that a proportion of the farming population at mid-nineteenth century was virtually "invisible" but contributed to the yields of the producing farmers of the state.

The third and fourth samples used are, strictly speaking, not samples at all. The third data set is composed of all the extant persistence rates collected from the social science literature in the last two decades. For a full description of these data, see Chapter 2. Finally, the bankruptcy data set consisted of a collection of all the extant bankruptcies between 1857 and 1859 listed in the Lewis County court records. These cases of bankruptcy were then hand linked to the 1855 New York State Census agricultural and population schedules (see Chapter 5).

PRIMARY SAMPLING UNITS

1855 Population Sample: Counties

Albany	Greene	Orange
Broome	Herkimer	Orleans
Cattaraugus	Jefferson	Oswego
Chemung	Livingston	Rensselaer
Chenango	Madison	Saratoga
Delaware	Monroe	Schoharie
Erie	Onondaga	Ulster
Essex	Ontario	Washington

Linked Farmer Sample: Counties and Towns

Broome County	Lewis County	Washington County
Nanticoke	Croham	Argyle
Union	Lowville	Ft. Edward
Windsor	New Bremen	Greenwich
Cattaraugus County	Monroe County	Yates County
Ashford	Clarkson	Barrington
Farmersville	Mumford	Benton
New Albion	Union Hall	Middlesex
Greene County	Onondaga County	
Cairo	Camillus	
Coxsackie	Fabius	
Durham	Lysander	

Commercialization Formula, 1855 and 1865

(expressed in bushels of corn equivalents)

LIVESTOCK

$(((A)*(D)*(E)/(F))-(A)*(G))^1 +$
$(((B)*(D)*(E)/(F))-(B)*(G))^2 +$
$(((C)*(D)*(E)/(F))-(C)*(G))^3 -$
$((H)*(G)) -$
$((I)*(G)) -$
$((J)*(G)) -$
$((L)*(G))^4 -$
$((K)*(G))^5 -$
$((M)*(G))^6 +$
$((N)/(O))-(((N)/(P))*(G))^7 +$

FIELD CROPS

$((Q)-((Q)*(CCC))) +$
$((R)-((R)*(CCC))) +$
$((S)-((S)*(CCC))) +$
$((T)-((T)*(CCC))) +$
$((U)-((U)*(CCC))) +$
$((V)-((V)*(CCC))) +$
$((W)-((W)*(CCC))) +$
$((X)-((X)*(CCC)))^8 +$
$(((Y)-((Y)*(CCC)))/(DDD)) +$
$(((Z)-((Z)*(CCC)))/(DDD)) +$
$(((AA)-((AA)*(CCC)))/(DDD))^9 +$
$(((BB)-((BB)*(CCC)))/(O))^{10} +$

DAIRY

$((CC)/(EEE)) +$
$((DD)/(EEE)) +$
$((EE)/(EEE))^{11} +$
$((FF)/(O))^{12} +$

MISCELLANEOUS

$((GG)/(O)) +$
$((HH)/(O)) +$
$((II)/(O)) +$
$((JJ)/(O)) +$
$((KK)/(O)) +$
$((LL)/(O)) +$
$((MM)/(O)) +$
$((NN)/(O)) +$
$((OO)/(O)) +$
$((PP)/(O)) +$
$((QQ)/(O)) +$
$(((GGG)-((GGG)*(CCC)))/(O)) +$
$((RR)/(O)) +$
$((SS)/(O)) +$
$((TT)/(O)) +$
$((UU)/(O)) +$
$((VV)/(O))^{13} -$

HUMAN CONSUMPTION

$(((WW)*(ZZ))*(AAA)) +$
$(((YY)-(WW))*(ZZ))*(BBB)^{14}$

Commercialization Formula Key—
1855 and 1865

A	Beef cattle consumed[1]
B	Swine (under six months) consumed[2]
C	Swine (over six months) consumed[3]
D	Weight estimate
E	Dressed meat proportion
F	Dressed meat, corn equivalent
G	Feed requirements
H	Neat cattle (under one year)[4]
I	Neat cattle (over one year)
J	Working oxen
K	Working cows[5]
L	Horses
M	Sheep[6]
N	Poultry value[7]
O	Corn price/conversion factor
P	Price per chicken
Q	Spring wheat (Bu)[8]
R	Winter wheat (Bu)[8]
S	Barley (Bu)[8]
T	Buckwheat (Bu)[8]
U	Peas (Bu)[8]
V	Beans (Bu)[8]
W	Corn (Bu)
X	Oats (Bu)[8]
Y	Rye (Bu)[9]
Z	Potatoes (Bu)[9]
AA	Turnips (Bu)[9]
BB	Hops (lbs)[10]
CC	Cheese (lbs)[11]
DD	Butter (lbs)[11]
EE	Milk (gals)[11]

FF	Eggs ($ value)[12]
GG	Apples (Bu)
HH	Market garden ($ value)
II	Maple syrup (lbs)
JJ	Maple molasses (gals)
KK	Wine (gals)
LL	Honey (lbs)
MM	Wax (lbs)
NN	Silk (lbs)
OO	Unenumerated articles ($ value)[13]
PP	Wool (lbs)
QQ	Other miscellaneous ($ value)
RR	Fulled cloth (yards)
SS	Flannel (yards)
TT	Linen (yards)
UU	Cotton cloth (yards)
VV	Other cloth (yards)
WW	Children in household
XX	Adults in household
YY	People in household
ZZ	Bushels of corn necessary to feed an adult male (one year)[14]
AAA	Children consumption factor[14]
BBB	Adult consumption factor[14]
CCC	Seed requirements
DDD	Grain calorie conversion factor
EEE	Dairy calorie conversion factor
FFF	Pounds to gallons conversion factor
GGG	Hay (tons)

Notes to Appendix 2 appear at the end of the Note Section.

Notes

CHAPTER 1

1. Richard Hofstadter, *The Age of Reform: From Bryan to FDR* (New York: Vintage Books, 1955).

2. Recognizing this unbridled nationalism, Alexis de Tocqueville noted with some dismay that "nothing is more annoying ... than this irritable patriotism of Americans." Alexis de Tocqueville, *Democracy in America* (New York: Vintage Books, 1945), 105.

3. On the contributions of the "great men" of this era to agricultural technology, for example, see Clarence H. Danhof, "The Tools and Implements of Agriculture," *Agricultural History* 46 (January 1972); Tocqueville, *Democracy in America*, 105; Bidwell and Falconer commented briefly on the growing materialism of rural folk, though interestingly, they focused on farm daughters: "the wants of the farm family were expanding rapidly ... the farmers' daughters wanted better clothes and pianos like those of their city cousins." Percy Bidwell and John Falconer, *History of Agriculture in the Northern States: 1620–1860*. Reprint. (New York: Peter Smith, [1925] 1941), 253.

4. For a full discussion of the effects of depopulation in New England, see Hal Seth Barron, "The Impact of Rural Depopulation on the Local Economy," *Agricultural History* 54 (April 1980); Hal Seth Barron, *Those Who Stayed Behind: Rural Society in Nineteenth Century New England* (New York: Cambridge University Press, 1984). The pioneering historical analysis assessing the relationship between migration and agricultural change was James Malin's "The Turnover of Farm Population in Kansas," *Kansas Historical Quarterly* 4 (1935): 339–72. Reprinted in Robert Swierenga, ed., *History and Ecology: Studies of Grassland* (Lincoln: University of Nebraska Press, 1984).

5. Louis Hartz, *The Liberal Tradition in America* (New York: Harcourt Brace, 1955); Daniel Boorstin, *The Genius of American Politics* (Chicago: University of Chicago Press, 1953); Richard Hofstadter, *The Progressive Historians* (New York: Vintage Books, 1968).

6. Christopher Clark, "The Household Economy, Market Exchange and the Rise of Capitalism in the Connecticut Valley, 1800–1860," *Journal of Social History* 13 (1979): 169–89; Christopher Clark, *The Roots of Rural Capitalism: Western Massachusetts, 1780–1860,* (Ithaca: Cornell University Press, 1990); Michael Merrill, "Cash is Good to Eat: Self-Sufficiency and Exchange in the Rural Economy of the United States," *Radical History Review* 3 (1977): 43–71; Robert E. Mutch, "The Transition to Capitalism," *Theory and Society* 9 (November 1980): 847–63; Thomas Dublin, "Women and Outwork in a Nineteenth Century New England Town," in Steven Hahn and Jonathan Prude, eds., *The Countryside in the*

Age of Capitalist Transformation (Chapel Hill: University of North Carolina Press, 1985) 51–69; Robert Swierenga, "Theoretical Perspectives on the New Rural History: From Environmentalism to Modernization," *Agricultural History* 56 (January 1982). For a discussion of the new rural history, see the introduction of Hahn and Prude, *The Countryside in the Age of Capitalist Transformation.* For the *homo economicus* quote, see Elizabeth Perkins, "The Consumer Frontier: Household Consumption in Early Kentucky," *Journal of American History* 78 (September 1991): 487; Winifred Rothenberg, *From Market-Place to a Market Economy* (Chicago: University of Chicago Press, 1992).

7. For a discussion of changes in agricultural commodity prices from 1840 to 1860, see Bidwell and Falconer, *History of Agriculture,* 504. For a full price series, see U.S. Bureau of Census, *Historical Statistics: Colonial Times to 1957* (Washington, D.C.: U.S. GPO, 1960), Series E 1-12, Wholesale Price Indexes (Warren and Pearson). For a comprehensive index that disaggregates farm crop and derivatives from industrial consumer goods, see *Historical Statistics,* Series E-68, Wholesale Price Index (Bezanson). Also see Jeremy Atack and Fred Bateman, *To Their Own Soil: Agriculture in the Antebellum North* (Ames: Iowa State University Press, 1987), for price estimates of particular agricultural products in 1859 and 1860, Table 13.1, 233, and see S.E. Ronk, *Prices of Farm Products in New York State, 1841 to 1935* (Ithaca: Cornell University Agricultural Station No. 643, 1936).

8. On rural consumption of manufactured goods, see Fred Bateman, "The 'Marketable Surplus' in Northern Dairy Farming: New Evidence by Size of Farm in 1860," *Agricultural History* 52 (July 1978): 345 (see his note 1).

9. Tamara Hareven, "The History of the Family and the Complexity of Social Change," *American Historical Review* 96 (February 1991): 117. Although Hareven's comments on consumption patterns were not directed toward this particular question, they are, as usual, very suggestive.

10. *Historical Statistics of the U.S.,* Series p 1-10, 409; House Document No. 136 in *Andrews' Report on Colonial and Lake Trade, 1852* (Washington, D.C., 1853): 698. The number of manufacturing establishments increased 104 percent from 123,025 to 252,148. Value added by manufacturing during this period increased 201 percent from $463,983 to $1,395,119, and manufacturing employees increased from 957,059 to 2,053,996. By 1850 New Yorkers had invested $99,904,059 in manufacturing, with an annual product of $237,597,249.

11. For a discussion of these price trends see, Dorothy Brady, "Relative Prices in the Nineteenth Century," *Journal of Economic History* 24 (1964); Dorothy Brady, "Consumption and Style of Life," in Lance Davis, Richard Easterlin, and William Parker, eds. *American Economic Growth: An Economist's History of the United States* (New York: Harper and Row, 1972). For an analysis of the "American System of Manufacturing" from two distinct historiographical perspectives, see David A. Houndshell, *From American System to Mass Production, 1800–1837: The Development of Manufacturing Technology in the United States* (Baltimore: Johns Hopkins University Press, 1984), and Donald R. Hoke, *Ingenious Yankees: The Rise of the American System of Manufactures in the Private Sector* (New York: Columbia University Press, 1990). On the role of rural peddlers, see David Jaffee, "Peddlers of Progress and the Transformation of the Rural North," *Journal of American History* 78 (September 1991): 511–35.

12. Lois Green Carr and Lorena S. Walsh, "Inventories and the Analysis of Wealth and Consumption Patterns in St. Mary's County, Maryland, 1658–1779," *Historical Methods* 13 (Spring 1980): 81–104; Lois Green and Lorena Walsh, "Toward a History of the Standard of Living in British North America," *William and Mary Quarterly* 45 (January 1988): 116–70.

13. Perkins, "The Consumer Frontier." For these changes compare the figures in Tables 1 and 4, pages 491 and 500. Although some of this increase would be expected in the normal

maturing process of a frontier community, Perkins' findings are still important.

14. Jaffee, "Peddlers of Progress." On page 522 Jaffee notes an increase in the number of peddlers listed in the U.S. Census from 10,669 in 1850 to 16,594 in 1860.

15. Tocqueville, *Democracy in America,* 210.

16. Ibid., 212.

17. Ibid., 212.

18. Benjamin Gue, *The Diary of Benjamin Gue,* August 21, 1851. New York State Library Collections, Albany, N.Y.

19. Ibid., November 8-10, 1848. It is interesting to note that Ben's rather casual reference to buying books suggests a distinct shift in their purchase from early nineteenth century Kentucky when only 4 percent of the probate inventories mentioned books. See Perkins, "Household Consumption," Table 4, page 500.

20. William Van Orden, *Account Book of William Van Orden,* April and May, 1860. New York State Library Collections, Albany, N.Y.

21. Isaac Phillips Roberts, *Autobiography of a Farm Boy* (Ithaca: Cornell University Press, 1946), 30 (originally published in 1916).

22. Tocqueville, *Democracy in America,* 212.

23. For a discussion of the shortage in agricultural labor during this period, see Bidwell and Falconer, *History of Agriculture,* especially Chapter XVI. The most comprehensive study of the effect of military land bounties during this period is James Oberly, *Ten Million Acres* (Kent, Ohio: Kent State University Press, 1989).

24. *The Northern Farmer,* January 1857: IV, 1, 5.

25. For example, the lead article of the November 1848 issue of *The Cultivator,* 329–30, was titled "Implements of the Late State Fair." In it the editors waxed enthusiastically, in more than 2400 words plus illustrations, about seed-sowers ... cultivators, plows, corn shellers, hay and manure forks, harvesting machines, mowing machines, fanning mills, churns, cheese presses, straw and corn stalk cutters, and portable mills. Also see Danhof, "The Tools and Implements of Agriculture."

26. William Van Orden, *Account Books,* March 1859. For a discussion of farm machinery purchases in Iowa during this period, see Allan Bogue, *From Prairie to Cornbelt* (Chicago: University of Chicago Press, 1963), Table 27, 226.

27. Peter Temin, *The Jacksonian Economy* (New York: Norton, 1969). For recent studies of the panic of 1857, see Charles W. Calomiris and Larry Schweikart, "The Panic of 1857: Origins, Transmission, and Containment," *Journal of Economic History* 51 (December 1991): 807–34, and James Huston, *The Panic of 1857 and the Coming of the Civil War* (Baton Rouge: Louisiana State University Press, 1987).

28. The bitter irony of this and other financial panics was that as land prices fell and farmers were pushed off their land, others were able to either move into farming or consolidate their holdings. As usual, economic change was a double-edged sword.

29. *The Genesee Farmer,* 1838, VII.

30. Bidwell and Falconer, *History of Agriculture,* 206.

31. Whitney Cross, *The Burned-Over District* (Ithaca: Cornell University Press, 1950), 141.

32. For a good introduction to agricultural journalism during this period, see Donald Marti "Agricultural Journalism and the Diffusion of Knowledge: The First Half Century in America," *Agricultural History* 54 (January 1980): 28–37. Also see Bidwell and Falconer, *History of Agriculture,* especially Chapter XXV.

33. For a good discussion of some of the "crazes" during this period, see Bidwell and Falconer, *History of Agriculture.* For examples of "bad advice" from agricultural journals, see Richard Wines, "The Nineteenth Century Agricultural Transition in an Eastern Long Island

Community," *Agricultural History* 55 (January 1981): 50–63.

34. *The Cultivator,* December 1851, VIII, 12, 385.

35. *The Cultivator,* January 1848, V, 1, 14.

36. *The Cultivator,* January 1848, V, 1, 13.

37. *The Cultivator,* January 1848, V, 1, 31. Speech by Mr. Payson to the Essex County Agricultural Society.

38. For a discussion of the residual issue in estimating nominal record linkage, see Donald Parkerson, "How Mobile Were Nineteenth Century Americans?" *Historical Methods* 15 (Summer 1982): 99–109.

39. Tocqueville, *Democracy in America.*

40. Although the index created here is a continuous measure of net production, I often refer to those farmers producing a surplus and those who do not. This distinction was a heuristic device used to help readers understand differences in the kinds of farmers that existed at mid-nineteenth century. There are, of course, real dangers in what might be seen in dichotomizing human behavior. However, while it is clear that virtually all farmers at this time had some involvement with the marketplace, there were important differences between them as well. Some were actively engaged in market activity, some were only marginally involved, and others were isolated from the cash economy. The heuristic model created here is based on a simple empirical reality: agricultural production. If the farmer produced enough food to feed his family and supply his farm with some product left over (surplus), he was categorized as a surplus market producer. If, on the other hand, his production was not sufficient to feed his family at an accepted standard of nutrition (measured in calories), he was classified as a yeoman. Again, although this model is not without its problems, its intention was to assist the reader in the analysis of these farmers and not to create an artificial dichotomy. See Chapter 5 for a further discussion of this issue.

41. J. Rikoon, *Threshing in the Midwest* (Bloomington: Indiana University Press, 1988), emphasizes the importance of culture in the transition to mechanized agriculture in the Midwest. Also see Atack and Bateman, *To Their Own Soil,* for an important discussion of the "cultural" component of Northern agriculture in 1860.

CHAPTER 2

1. Michel Chevalier, *Society, Manners, and Politics in the United States,* John W. Ward, ed. (Garden City: Doubleday, 1961), 286.

2. Alexis de Tocqueville, *Democracy in America* (New York: Vintage Books, 1945), 130.

3. Ibid., 183.

4. Ibid., 193. Throughout this discussion, Tocqueville compares America to "aristocratic" nations.

5. Ibid., 193.

6. The literature on the methodology of nominal record linkage is substantial. Some important early research includes Ian Winchester, "The Linkage of Historical Records by Man and Computer: Techniques and Problems," *Journal of Interdisciplinary History* (Autumn 1970): 107–25; Myron Gutmann, "The Future of Record Linkage in History," *Journal of Family History* 2 (1977): 151–57; Michael Katz and J. Tiller, "Record Linkage for Everyman: A Semi-Automated Process," *Historical Methods* 5 (1975): 144–50; Charles Stephenson, "Tracing Those Who Left: Mobility Studies and the Sound Indexes to the U.S. Census," *Journal of Urban History* 1 (1977): 73–84. For some excellent applications of the methodology of nominal record linkage, see Peter Knights, *Yankee Destinies* (Chapel Hill: University of North Carolina Press, 1991); various papers and a forthcoming book by anthropologists John Adams

and Alice Kasakoff including, "Migration and the Family in Colonial New England: The View from Genealogies," *The Journal of Family History* 9 (Spring 1984): 24–43. Also see the extensive work of Gerard Bouchard and his colleagues at the Université du Québec à Chicoutimi. See SOREP (Inter-University Centre for Population Research) *Annual Reports,* by Gerard Bouchard, Director, Université du Québec à Chicoutimi.

7. W.R. Prest, "Stability and Change in Old and New England: Clayworth and Dedham," *Journal of Interdisciplinary History* 6 (Winter 1976): 359–74. In order to test the null hypothesis that community size had no effect on the persistence rate of a community, I examined, in a meta-analysis, persistence rates published in scholarly journals and books. The unit of analysis was the particular community under study; characteristics of the community became independent variables; the persistence rate became the dependent variable. Variations in these rates then were examined in the context of each of these community characteristics. I found that none of these variables was significant. In short, the size of a community was not related systematically to variations in persistence in the past. For a full discussion of the technique of meta-analysis as well as the community characteristics examined, see Donald Parkerson, "How Mobile Were Nineteenth Century Americans?" *Historical Methods* 15 (Summer 1982): 99–109.

8. Stanley Lebergott, "Migration within the U.S., 1800–1960: Some New Estimates," *Journal of Economic History* 30 (1970): 839–46.

9. This analysis of migration is based on the 1855 "population sample" (see Appendix 1). It is a stratified/random sample of rural and urban New Yorkers (except New York City) at least fifteen years of age. Most other analyses in this volume are based on what I have called the "linked sample." See Appendix 1 for a complete discussion of samples and sampling strategies.

10. Joseph Smith, *New York Manuscript Census, 1855.* Livingston County, N.Y.

11. Benjamin Gue, *Diary of Benjamin Gue,* January 1, 1852, 155. New York State Library Collections, Albany, N.Y.

12. Ibid.

13. Michael Katz, Michael Doucet, and Mark Stern, "Migration and the Social Order in Erie County, New York, 1855," *Journal of Interdisciplinary History* 8 (1978):669–702.

14. John O'Brien and Gilbert Jones, *New York State Manuscript Census, 1855.* Rensselaer County, N.Y. O'Brien and Jones, *New York State Manuscript Census, 1865,* Rensselaer County, N.Y.

15. Peter Knights, for example, has recognized the enormous difficulties in tracing ethnic people in the nineteenth century and as a result decided to focus on native whites in his *Yankee Destinies.* Although Knights has been criticized for this decision, he has produced the most comprehensive study of urban migration to date. For a discussion of how record linkage problems inflate our estimates of migration, especially in rapidly expanding cities, see Parkerson, "How Mobile Were Nineteenth Century Americans?" For a discussion of census underenumeration in the nineteenth century, see the articles in a special issue of *Social Science History* 15 (1991): 509–602.

16. Oscar Handlin, *The Uprooted* (Boston: Little, Brown, 1951).

17. Emilene Austin, *New York State Manuscript Census, 1855.* Rensselaer County, N.Y.

18. James Burton, *New York State Manuscript Census, 1855.* Sullivan County, N.Y.

19. Michael Anderson, *Family Structure in Nineteenth Century Lancashire* (Cambridge, U.K.: Cambridge University Press, 1971).

20. Thomas Ross household, William Ross, Sr., household, *New York State Manuscript Census, 1855.* Fulton County, N.Y.

21. William Wort, *New York State Manuscript Census, 1855.* Jefferson County, N.Y.; Ansel Cushman, *New York State Manuscript Census, 1855.* Saratoga County, N.Y.

22. George Ballard and Francis Foster, *New York State Manuscript Census, 1855.* Broome County, N.Y.; Ballard and Foster, *New York State Manuscript Census, 1865.* Broome County, N.Y.

CHAPTER 3

1. Vernon Louis Parrington, *Main Currents in American Thought* (New York: Harcourt Brace, 1954), Volume I, vi, vii; Volume II, vii.

2. Ferdinand Tönnies' classic distinction between "gemeinschaft" and "gesellschaft" is a good introduction to these ideas. See Ferdinand Tönnies, *Community and Society*, Charles Loomis, ed. (East Lansing: Michigan State University Press, 1957); Georg Simmel, *The Sociology of Georg Simmel*, Kurt Wolff, ed. (New York: The Free Press, 1950), 422.

3. Simmel, *The Sociology of Georg Simmel*, 404.

4. Ibid., 422.

5. Robert E. Park, Ernest Burgess, and Roderick McKenzie, *The City* (Chicago: University of Chicago Press, 1925).

6. Benjamin Malzberg, "Migration and Mental Disease Among Negroes in New York State," *American Journal of Physical Anthropology* 2 (January 1936): 107–13; Malzberg, "Rates of Mental Disease Among Certain Populations in New York State," *Journal of the American Statistical Association* 31 (September 1936): 547.

7. Ronald Freedman, "Health Differentials for Rural-Urban Migration," *American Sociological Review* 12 (1974): 536–41.

8. W.I. Thomas and Florien Znanecki, *The Polish Peasant in Europe and America* (Boston: R.G. Badger, 1918).

9. Ernest R. Mowrer and Pauline Young, "The Reorganization of the Jewish Family Life in America: A Natural History of Social Forces Governing the Assimilation of the Jewish Immigrant," *Social Forces* (December 1928): 213–43.

10. Oscar Handlin, *The Uprooted* (Boston: Little, Brown, 1951).

11. Harvey J. Locke, "Mobility and Family Disorganization," *American Sociological Review* 5 (August 1940): 492–93.

12. Alexis de Tocqueville, *Democracy in America* (New York: Vintage Books, 1945), 194.

13. Frederick Jackson Turner, "The Significance of the Frontier in American History," in *The Turner Thesis Concerning the Role of the Frontier in American History*, George Rogers Taylor, ed. (Boston: Heath, 1941). Also see Turner, *Rise of the New West* (New York: Harper and Bros., 1906).

14. George Pierson, *The Moving American* (New York: Knopf, 1973), 48.

15. Everett Lee, "The Turner Thesis Reexamined," *American Quarterly* 13 (Spring 1961): 77–83.

16. Thomas Cochran, *Frontiers of Change: Early Industrialization in America,* (New York: Oxford University Press, 1981), 14.

17. Alex Inkles and David Smith, *Becoming Modern* (Cambridge, U.K.: Cambridge University Press, 1974).

18. H.G. Barnett, *Innovations: The Basis of Cultural Change* (New York: McGraw-Hill, 1953).

19. Simmel, *The Sociology of Georg Simmel*, 404.

20. Cochran, *Frontiers of Change.*

21. Chevalier, *Society, Manners, and Politics,* 286.

22. Cochran, *Frontiers of Change.*

23. Thomas Jefferson, *Notes on Virginia,* 1794, reprinted in Richard Hofstadter, *Great Issues in American History,* Volume 2 (New York: Vintage, 1958), 169–70.

24. Pierson, *The Moving American*, 48.

25. Ibid.

26. Ibid.

27. Quoted in Eric Monkkonen, ed., "Introduction." *Walking to Work: Tramps in America, 1790–1935* (Lincoln: University of Nebraska Press, 1984), 15.

28. Stephan Thernstrom, *Poverty and Progress: Social Mobility in a Nineteenth Century City* (Cambridge, Mass: Harvard University Press, 1964). While Merle Curti discovered high rates of population turnover in Trempleau County, Wisconsin, during the nineteenth century, his work did not have the same impact on the field as did Thernstrom's just five years later. See Merle Curti, *The Making of an American Community: A Case Study of Democracy in a Frontier County* (Stanford: Stanford University Press, 1959). Of course, the pioneering study of population turnover in rural communities was James C. Malin, "The Turnover of Farm Population in Kansas," *Kansas Historical Quarterly* 4 (1935): 339–72. Reprinted in Robert Swierenga, ed., *History and Ecology: Studies of the Grassland* (Lincoln: University of Nebraska Press, 1984).

29. Peter Knights, *The Plain People of Boston, 1830–1860: A Study in City Growth* (New York: Oxford University Press, 1971). For an important follow-up study to this work, see his *Yankee Destinies*.

30. Michael Katz, *The People of Hamilton, Canada West: Family and Class in a Mid-Nineteenth Century City* (Cambridge, U.K.: Cambridge University Press, 1975), 17.

31. Michael Katz, Michael Doucet, and Mark Stern, "Migration and the Social Order in Erie County, New York, 1855," *Journal of Interdisciplinary History* 8 (1978): 669–702.

32. Robert Barrows, "Hurryin' Hoosiers and the American 'Pattern': Geographic Mobility in Indianapolis and Urban North America," *Social Science History* 5 (1980): 197–222.

33. Frank Furstenburg, Douglas Strong, and Albert G. Crawford, "What Happened When the Census Was Redone: An Analysis of the Recount of 1870 in Philadelphia," *Sociology and Social Research* 61 (1979): 475–505.

34. Ibid.

35. Ansley Coale and Melvin Zelnik, *New Estimates of Fertility and Population in the United States: A Study of Annual White Births from 1855 to 1960 and the Completeness of Enumeration in the Census from 1880 to 1960* (Princeton: Princeton University Press, 1963).

36. See the series of articles on census underenumeration in a special issue of *Social Science History* 15 (1991): 509–692.

37. Ibid.

38. For a brief summary of the new research on underenumeration in the U.S. Census in the nineteenth century, see Donald H. Parkerson, "Comments on Underenumeration of the U.S. Census, 1850–1880," *Social Science History* 15 (1991): 509–19.

39. Peter Knights and Richard S. Alcorn, "Most Uncommon Bostonians: A Critique of Stephan Thernstrom's *The Other Bostonians: Poverty and Progress in the American Metropolis: 1850–1970*," *Historical Methods* 8 (Fall 1975): 98–114. As noted in Chapter 2, Knights recognized the "common name problem" in nominal record linkage and eliminated immigrants from his sample of male Bostonians in his *Yankee Destinies*.

40. *New York State Manuscript Census, 1855*.

41. Donald H. Parkerson, "How Mobile Were Nineteenth Century Americans?" *Historical Methods* 15 (Summer 1982): 99–109.

42. Ibid.

43. These calculations are derived from Donald Parkerson and Jo Ann Parkerson, "Estimating the Population Dynamics of New York State at Mid-Nineteenth Century: A Group-Event Approach." Paper presented at the Social Science History Association Meetings, Chicago, 1989 (available from the authors).

44. Tocqueville, *Democracy in America*, 536.

CHAPTER 4

1. Richard Hofstadter, *The Age of Reform: From Bryan to FDR* (New York: Vintage Books, 1955).

2. Ibid., 23.

3. James T. Lemon, "Household Consumption in Eighteenth Century America and its Relationship to Production and Trade: The Situation Among Farmers in Southeastern Pennsylvania," *Agricultural History* 41 (January 1967): 59–70.

4. Douglass North, *The Economic Growth of the United States, 1790–1860,* (Englewood Cliffs, N.J.: Prentice Hall, 1961).

5. Albert Fishlow, "Antebellum Interregional Trade Reconsidered," in Ralph L. Andreano, ed., *New Views on American Economic Development* (Cambridge, Mass: Schenkman Publishing Co., 1965).

6. Percy Bidwell and John Falconer, *History of Agriculture in the Northern States: 1620–1860*. Reprint (New York: Peter Smith, [1925] 1941), 162, 165.

7. James Henretta "Families and Farm: Mentalite in Pre-Industrial America," *William and Mary Quarterly,* 3rd Series, 35 (January 1978): 3–32.

8. Christopher Clark, "The Household Economy, Market Exchange and the Rise of Capitalism in the Connecticut Valley, 1800–1860," *Journal of Social History* 13 (Fall 1979): 169–89. Christopher Clark, *The Roots of Rural Capitalism, Western Massachusetts, 1780–1860,* (Ithaca: Cornell University Press, 1990); Michael Merrill, "Cash is Good to Eat: Self-Sufficiency and Exchange in the Rural Economy of the United States," *Radical History Review* 3 (1977): 43–71; Robert E. Mutch, "The Cutting Edge: Colonial America and the Debate About the Transition to Capitalism," *Theory and Society* 9 (1980): 847–63; Thomas Dublin, "Women and Outwork in a Nineteenth Century New England Town," in Steven Hahn and Jonathan Prude, eds., *The Countryside in the Age of Capitalist Transformation* (Chapel Hill: University of North Carolina Press, 1985): 51–69; for a good general discussion of the new rural history see the introduction of Hahn and Prude, *The Countryside in the Age of Capitalist Transformation*. Finally, for a discussion of the question of self-sufficiency, see Bettye Hobbs Pruitt "Self-Sufficiency and the Agricultural Economy of Massachusetts," *William and Mary Quarterly* 41 (July 1984): 333–64.

9. Clark, "The Household Economy."

10. Merrill, "Cash is Good to Eat."

11. Pruitt "Self-Sufficiency," 338.

12. Winifred Rothenberg, *From Market-Place to a Market Economy* (Chicago: University of Chicago Press, 1992), 48, 53.

13. Pruitt, "Self Sufficiency"; Alan Taylor, *Liberty Men and Great Proprietors* (Chapel Hill: University of North Carolina Press, 1990); also see Porter Bliss, *Diary of Porter Bliss, 1854,* Bliss Family Papers, New York State Library Collections, Albany, N.Y.

14. Taylor, *Liberty Men and Great Proprietors,* 77.

15. Lemon, "Household Consumption," 68.

16. Ibid.

17. Ibid., Table II, 69.

18. Ibid., 68, note 52.

19. Ibid., 69.

20. U.S. Bureau of the Census, *Historical Statistics of the U.S,* Series Z-388-405 (Washington, D.C.: U.S. GPO, 1961), "Basic Weekly Diets in Britain and America: 1622–1790," 774.

21. Carole Shammas, "The Eighteenth Century English Diet and Economic Change," *Explorations in Economic History* 21 (July 1984): 254–69. For a broader interpretation, see

Shammas, *The Pre-Industrial Consumer in England and America* (Oxford: Oxford University Press, 1990); Robert Fogel, "Biomedical Approaches to the Estimation and Interpretation of Secular Trends in Equity, Morbidity, Mortality and Labor Productivity in Europe, 1750–1980," (University of Chicago, 1987, mimeographed), cited in Geert Bekaert, "Caloric Consumption in Industrializing Belgium," *Journal of Economic History* 51 (September 1991): Table 3, 639. Also see Cormac Ó. Gráda, *Ireland: A New Economic History, 1780–1939* (Oxford: Oxford University Press, 1994), cited in Bekaert, Table 3, 639; John Komlos, *Nutrition and Economic Development in the Eighteenth Century Habsburg Monarchy: An Anthropometric History,* (Princeton: Princeton University Press, 1990); Bekaert, "Caloric Consumption," 652.

22. For a review of the "entrepreneurial school," which emphasizes early and widespread commercialization, see Joyce Appleby, "Commercial Farming and the 'Agrarian Myth' in the Early Republic," *Journal of American History* 48 (1982): 833–35. Also see Pruitt "Self-Sufficiency."

23. Bekaert, "Caloric Consumption in Belgium," 652; Jeremy Atack and Fred Bateman, *To Their Own Soil: Agriculture in the Antebellum North* (Ames: Iowa State University Press, 1987); Marvin McInnis "Marketable Surpluses in Ontario Farming," *Social Science History* 8 (Fall 1984): 395–424. For an excellent overview of dietary changes of Americans, see Harvey Levenstein, *Revolution at the Table: The Transformation of the American Diet* (New York: Oxford University Press, 1988).

24. William Thompson, *A Tradesman's Travels in the United States and Canada* (Edinburgh: Oliver and Boyd, 1842), 125.

25. James Stuart, *Three Years in North America* (Edinburgh: R. Cadell, 1833), 42.

26. John Howison, *Sketches of Upper Canada: Domestic, Local, and Characteristics and Some Recollections of the United States of America* (Edinburgh: S.R. Publishers, 1822), 310.

27. Edward Thomas Coke, *A Subaltern's Furlough: Description of Scenes in Various Parts of the United States During the Summer and Autumn of 1832* (New York: J.J. Harper, 1833), 15; some suggestion of farmers' greater consumption of dairy products comes from Fred Bateman, "The Marketable Surplus in Northern Dairy Farming: New Evidence by Size of Farm in 1860," *Agricultural History* 52 (July 1978): 354. He notes that "farm families traditionally consumed larger quantities of milk and dairy products than did the non-farm population." He also cites (with some caution) Silas Loomis' estimate that milk consumption in New York City was only one-half of that in the countryside.

28. Dublin, "Women and Outwork."

29. *Diary of William Holbrook,* 1854 New York State Library Collections, Albany, N.Y.

30. Ulysses Prentiss Hedrick, *A History of Agriculture in the State of New York* (Albany: New York State Agricultural Society, 1933).

31. Ibid.

32. Dorothy Brady, "Relative Prices in the Nineteenth Century," *Journal of Economic History* 24 (June 1964): 145–203; barter equivalents can be found on Table 13; quote is on page 174.

33. Hedrick, *A History of Agriculture*; also see various issues of *The Northern Farmer, The Cultivator,* and *The Genesee Farmer* for discussions of "coopering."

34. Bliss, *Diary of Porter Bliss,* August and September 1854.

35. Ibid.

36. See various issues of *The Northern Farmer, The Cultivator,* and *The Genesee Farmer* for a discussion of wooden products and the market for them. Also see Hedrick, *A History of Agriculture,* 138.

37. *Diary of Rice Cook,* 1854. New York State Library Collections, Albany, N.Y.

38. Ibid.

39. See various issues of *The Northern Farmer, The Cultivator,* and *The Genesee Farmer.*

40. Bliss, *Diary of Porter Bliss,* July and August, 1854.

41. See Hedrick, *A History of Agriculture,* for a discussion of the Salina Salt Works and their demand for cordwood, 153. For estimates of the New York Central's demand for cordwood and the allocation of time in processing wood, see Paul Gates, "Problems of Agricultural History," *Agricultural History* 46 (January 1972): 37.

42. See various issues of *The Northern Farmer, The Cultivator,* and *The Genesee Farmer.* Also see Gates, "Problems of Agricultural History," for his estimates of time devoted to "preparing wood for various uses," 38.

43. Bliss, *Diary of Porter Bliss,* December 1854.

44. See Hedrick, *A History of Agriculture,* for a discussion of charcoal making, 143–44. For charcoal making in Connecticut, see Percy Bidwell, "The Agricultural Revolution in New England," *American Historical Review* 26 (July 1921): 697.

45. *Diary of Delos Hackley,* March and April 1862. I would like to thank Charles Mittlestadt, East Carolina University, for the use of these diaries.

46. For a discussion of maple syrup harvesting in the nineteenth century, see various issues of *The Northern Farmer* and *The Cultivator;* also see Hedrick, *A History of Agriculture,* 151–52, and *American Agriculturist* 39 (August 1870): 30, for a good discussion of this important industry.

47. John Hull, *New York State Manuscript Census, 1865,* Washington County, N.Y.

48. Abjah Ransom, *New York State Manuscript Census, 1865,* Washington County, N.Y.

49. Bliss, *Diary of Porter Bliss,* May 28, 1865.

50. Ibid., June 4, 1865.

51. Ibid., September 10, 1865.

52. Ibid., June 5, 1865.

53. Ibid., June 11 and 12, 1865.

54. Alexis de Tocqueville, *Democracy in America.* (New York: Vintage Books, 1945), 216.

55. Henry Dutchess household, *New York State Manuscript Census, 1855,* Yates County, N.Y.

56. Samuel Pitcher and George Robinson households, *New York State Manuscript Census, 1855,* Yates County, N.Y.

57. Robert Teneyck, *New York State Manuscript Census, 1855,* Yates County, N.Y.

58. Daniel Wing, *New York State Manuscript Census, 1855,* Yates County, N.Y.

59. William Norton, *New York State Manuscript Census, 1855,* Yates County, N.Y.

CHAPTER 5

1. *The Cultivator,* April 1852, IX, 4, 163.

2. Ibid.

3. *The Northern Farmer,* May 1857, IV, 5.

4. Ibid.

5. *The Cultivator,* December 1851, VIII, 12, 385.

6. Thomas Cochran, *Frontiers of Change: Early Industrialization in America* (New York: Oxford University Press, 1981).

7. *The Cultivator,* December 1851, VIII, 12, 385.

8. Speech by Professor Norton, Yale University, to the Washington County Fair, *The Cultivator,* November 1851, VIII, 11.

9. *The Cultivator,* June 1852, IX, 6, 205.

10. *The Northern Farmer,* January 1857, IV, 1, 24.

11. *The Northern Farmer,* June 1856, III, 6, 280–82.

12. *The Northern Farmer,* April 1857, IV, 4, 103.

13. Ibid.

14. *The Northern Farmer,* February 1857, IV, 2, 76.

15. Ibid.

16. Ibid.

17. *The Cultivator,* June 1852, IX, 6, 206.

18. Ibid.

19. *The Northern Farmer,* November 1856, III, 11, 524.

20. Ibid.

21. Nancy Grey Osterud, *Bonds of Community* (Ithaca: Cornell University Press, 1991).

22. Ibid., 168.

23. *Diaries of Delos Hackley,* 1855–68.

24. The critical reader might see as tautological comparisons of farm yields between "yeomen" farmers and "surplus market farmers" because production differences formed the basis of these heuristic categories (see note 40, Chapter 1). However, comparisons of farm yields were made simply to demonstrate the magnitude of these production differences. Other comparisons in this and other chapters will demonstrate that variations in farm yields were just one of many important differences between these two groups. These include crop and dairy yields per unit investment strategies, migration profiles, household structure, and fertility. Finally, it should be noted once again that these categories simply summarize net yield estimates measured at the interval level.

25. See the Agricultural Schedules of the 1855 and 1865 New York State Manuscript Census. It should be noted here that 1855 and 1865 generally were typical harvest years. With the exception of August 1855, rainfall totals were normal. See Franklin B. Hough, *Census of the State of New York for 1855* (Albany: Charles Van Benthurysen, 1857), liv–lv, for a discussion of the history of rainfall in New York State in the nineteenth century. Also see various issues of *The Cultivator* and *The Northern Farmer* for a discussion of harvests during these years. Finally, while many farmers during this period claimed that their yields were below "normal," this seems to be quite common among most farmers at this time.

26. Surplus market farmers also registered a sharp increase in their numbers who manufactured cheese between 1855 and 1865 (45.6 percent). The small number of cases here precluded further analysis. Similarly, although there were too few cases of milk producers in this sample to assess production changes over the decade, it is apparent that by the end of the Civil War an increasing number of commercially minded farmers with access to urban markets were beginning to serve local townsfolk with fresh milk.

27. Henry Dutchess, Samuel Pitcher, and George Robinson, *New York State Manuscript Census, 1855,* Yates County, N.Y.

28. Lyman Hull, *New York State Manuscript Census, 1855,* Greene County, N.Y.; Lyman Hull, *New York State Manuscript Census, 1865,* Greene County, N.Y.

29. Lyman Hull, Levi Gilbert, John Hull, and Jonah Ransom, *New York State Manuscript Census, 1855,* Greene County, N.Y.; and *New York State Manuscript Census, 1865,* Greene County, N.Y.

30. Levi Gilbert, *New York State Manuscript Census, 1855,* Greene County, N.Y.; and *New York State Manuscript Census, 1865,* Greene County, N.Y.

CHAPTER 6

1. Hiram Odell, *New York State Manuscript Census, 1855,* Broome County, N.Y.

2. William Skillie, *New York State Census Manuscript Census, 1855,* Washington

County, N.Y. The diversified production of the Skillies was typical of many surplus market farmers in New York at mid-nineteenth century. Recently, Mary Eschelbach Gregson in her study of agriculture in Missouri during this period found that as farmers moved to the commercial economy they often diversified rather than specialized their production. See Mary Eschelbach Gregson, "Strategies for Commercialization: Missouri Agriculture, 1860–1880" (Ph.D. diss., University of Illinois at Urbana-Champaign, 1993).

3. Court records from Lewis County, N.Y., 1855–60, were hand linked to the *New York State Manuscript Census, 1855,* Lewis County, N.Y.

4. Ibid., John Malloy, Lewis County (census and court records linked).

5. Ibid., Nicholas Smith, Lewis County (census and court records linked).

6. Ibid., William Royce, Lewis County (census and court records linked).

7. In his classic article "The Turnover of Farm Population in Kansas," published in 1935, James C. Malin first dealt with the relationship between individual and community levels of migration in the context of agricultural change. He noted that at an early stage of agricultural development, there was a rapid population turnover but that as communities grew, migration declined. Finally, when a community matured, it became much more stable, with little out-migration. James C. Malin, "The Turnover of Farm Population in Kansas," *Kansas Historical Quarterly* 4 (1935): 339–72. Reprinted in Robert Swierenga, *History and Ecology: Studies of the Grassland* (Lincoln: University of Nebraska Press, 1984).

8. Ansel Cushman, *New York State Manuscript Census, 1855,* Washington County, N.Y.

9. Charles Murray, *New York State Manuscript Census, 1855,* Monroe County, N.Y.

10. Gilbert Jones, *New York State Manuscript Census, 1855,* Monroe County, N.Y.

11. William Gibson, *New York State Manuscript Census, 1855,* Washington County, N.Y.

12. John M. Barber and Henry Howe, *Historical Collections of the State of New York* (Port Washington, N.Y.: S. Tuttle, 1841).

13. Simon Crandall, *New York State Manuscript Census, 1855,* Washington County, N.Y.; *New York State Manuscript Census, 1865,* Washington County, N.Y.

14. William Wort, *New York State Manuscript Census, 1855,* Jefferson County, N.Y.

15. Barber and Howe, *Historical Collections,* 200.

16. N.G. Clark, *New York State Manuscript Census, 1855,* Monroe County, N.Y.

17. Hal Seth Barron, *Those Who Stayed Behind: Rural Society in Nineteenth Century New England* (New York: Cambridge University Press, 1984).

18. John Hopkins, John Moore, James Hanna, Hugh King, Joseph Patterson, William Lindsay, *New York State Manuscript Census, 1855,* Washington County, N.Y.; *New York State Manuscript Census, 1865,* Washington County, N.Y.

19. Once again, note the parallel findings of James C. Malin in his "The Turnover of Farm Population."

CHAPTER 7

1. The 1855 New York State Census recorded duration-of-residence information for each member of the household. As a result I was able to examine the in-migration of boarders or other relatives to the household. These data allow us to move beyond the "static" interpretation of households without longitudinal information. Without these kinds of data, all members of the household appear to have arrived in the community at the same time, creating the illusion of static household organization.

2. The literature on "progressive nucleation" is extensive. See, for example, Louis Wirth, "Urbanism as a Way of Life," *American Journal of Sociology* 45 (1943): 22–38; Tal-

cott Parsons, *Family Socialization and Interaction Process* (Glencoe, Ill.: Free Press 1955); William F. Ogburn, *Technology and the Changing Family* (Boston: Houghton Mifflin, 1955). Recently, Daniel Scott Smith has demonstrated that the progressive nucleation argument was not well articulated in the scholarly literature until the late 1930s and even by the mid-1950s was relatively unimportant. As a kind of "straw man," however, this theory has had a profound effect on those "revisionist" scholars who tried to demonstrate the ubiquity of the nuclear household from the end of the sixteenth century. See Daniel Scott Smith, "The Curious History of Theorizing About the History of the Western Nuclear Family," *Social Science History* 17 (1993): 325–53.

3. See Peter Laslett and Richard Wall, eds., *Household and Family in Past Time* (New York: Cambridge University Press, 1972). Using a typology developed in this work (p. 28–31), one would define the nuclear family (or conjugal family unit) as a couple plus offspring. The "extended family household" consists of the nuclear family plus additional relatives whose spouses and children, if they have them, do not cohabit. The "stem family," a special case of a "multiple family household," consists of a senior couple with a son and his bride who live with them, typically with an expectation of inheritance.

4. Edward Shorter, *The Making of the Modern Family* (New York: Basic Books, 1975), 30. As Steven Ruggles recently has noted, the "view that family structure has been stable for centuries in Northwestern Europe and the United States ... has had a crippling effect on the field"; Steven Ruggles, "The Transformation of American Family Structure," *American Historical Review* 99 (1994): 103–128. In fact, Tamara Hareven has shown that as a result, very few studies of family structure have been published since the late 1970s and early 1980s; Tamara Hareven, "The History of the Family and the Complexity of Social Change," *American Historical Review* 96 (1991): 95–124.

5. Tamara Hareven, "The Family as Process: The Historical Study of the Family Cycle," *Journal of Social History* 7 (Spring 1974): 322–29; Lutz Berkner, "The Stem Family and the Developmental Cycle of the Peasant Household: An Eighteenth-Century Austrian Example," *American Historical Review* 77 (April 1972): 398–418; Steven Ruggles, "Availability of Kin and the Demography of Historical Family Structure," *Historical Methods* 19 (Summer 1986): 93–102; Michael Anderson, *Family Structure in Nineteenth-Century Lancashire* (Cambridge: Cambridge University Press, 1971).

6. Rachel Wright, *New York State Manuscript Census, 1855,* Farmersville, N.Y.; George, Mary, and Orin Giles, *New York State Manuscript Census, 1855,* Argyle, N.Y.

7. E.G. Ravenstein, "The Laws of Migration: First Paper," *Journal of the Royal Statistical Society* 48 (1885); Ravenstein, "The Laws of Migration: Second Paper," *Journal of the Royal Statistical Society* 52 (1889); T.J. Courchene, "Interprovincial Migration and Economic Adjustment," *Canadian Journal of Economics* 3 (November 1970): 550–75; M.J. Greenwood and I. Gormerly, "A Comparison of the Determinants of White and Non-White Migration," *Demography* 8 (February 1971):141–55; Bernard Bass and Ralph Alexander, "Climate, Economy, and the Differential Migration of White and Non-White Workers," *Journal of Applied Psychology* 56 (1972): 518–21; P.M. Sommers and D.B. Suits, "Analysis of Net Interstate Migration," *Southern Economic Journal* 40 (October 1973): 193–201; James D. Tarver and William R. Gurley, "The Relationship of Selected Variables with County Net Migration Rates in the United States, 1950–1960," *Rural Sociology* 30 (March 1965): 3–13; Richard Raymond, "Determinants of Non-White Migration During the 1950s: Their Regional Significance and Long Term Implications," *American Journal of Economic Sociology* 31 (January 1972): 9–20; Wilbur Zelinsky, "The Hypothesis of the Mobility Transition," *Geographical Review* 61 (April 1971): 219–49; Frederick Jackson Turner, "The Significance of the Frontier in American History," in George Rogers Taylor, ed., *The Turner Thesis Concerning the Role of the Frontier in American History* (Boston: Heath, 1941).

8. J. Brown, H. Swarzweller, and J. Mangalam, "Kentucky Mountain Migration and the Stem Family: An American Variation on a Theme by LePlay," *Rural Sociology* 28 (March 1963): 48–69; J. MacDonald and L. MacDonald, "Chain Migration, Ethnic Neighborhood Formation, and Social Networks," *Milbank Memorial Fund Quarterly* 42 (January 1964): 82–93; Virginia Yans-McLaughlin, *Family and Community: Italian Immigrants in Buffalo, 1880–1930* (Ithaca: Cornell University Press, 1977); Gordon Darroch, "Migrants in the Nineteenth Century: Fugitives or Families in Motion?" *Journal of Family History* 6 (Fall 1981): 257–77; Herbert Gutman, *The Black Family in Slavery and Freedom: 1750–1925* (New York: Pantheon Books, 1976); Laurence Glasco, "Migration and Adjustment in the Nineteenth Century City: Occupation, Property, and Household Structure of Native Born Whites, Buffalo, New York, 1855," in Tamara Hareven and Maris Vinovskis, eds., *Family and Population in Nineteenth-Century America* (Princeton: Princeton University Press, 1978); Donald H. Parkerson, "The Changing Pattern of Internal Migration of Americans," paper presented to the Social Science History Association, 1982.

9. Jonah Ransom, *New York State Manuscript Census, 1855,* Greene County, N.Y.; and *New York State Manuscript Census, 1865,* Greene County.

10. In order to identify "relatives living nearby," I searched the population schedules for "same surname relatives" of the sample member, five dwellings in either direction. For example, if the sample farmer was listed in dwelling number 105, then I would search dwellings 100 through 104 and 106 through 110 for kin. Although not without problems, this technique provides a lower bound estimate of kin clustering because relatives from the matriarchal side could not be identified.

11. Lee Craig, "The Value of Household Labor in Antebellum Northern Agriculture," *Journal of Economic History* 51 (March 1991): 67–81, see Table 3, page 74. Also see Craig's new work *To Sow One Acre More* (Baltimore: Johns Hopkins University Press, 1993). These findings were replicated for 1855 and 1865 using the "Linked Farmer Sample." In both years, children in the household were associated with significantly lower net yields.

12. David Galenson, "Economic Determinants of the Age at Leaving Home: Evidence From the Lives of Nineteenth Century New England Manufacturers," *Social Science History* 11 (Winter 1987): 355–78.

13. Galenson, "Economic Determinants."

14. Anderson, *Family Structure.*

CHAPTER 8

1. For a recent discussion of the decline in migration, see Ronald Tobey, Charles Wetherell, and Jay Brigham, "Moving Out and Settling In: Residential Mobility, Homeowning, and the Public Enframing of Citizenship, 1921–1950," *American Historical Review* 95 (December 1990): 1395–1422. For a discussion of the mobility transition, see Chapter 2.

2. While migration clearly is a multidimensional demographic phenomenon consisting of the simultaneous processes of in- and out-migration (in addition to both the individual and community level perspectives), we typically use either the persistence rate or the net migration rate as our exclusive measure of population turnover. The persistence rate, of course, is useful in estimating the volume of out-migration from a community. But by focusing our attention exclusively on it, we tend to ignore the role of in-migration. It is for this reason that the continuous-years-of-residence data from the 1855 New York State Census are so valuable. Similarly, net migration rates, although useful as a summary measure, cannot distinguish between very mobile communities experiencing high in- and out-migration and those static communities with virtually no migration at all. Each of these types of communities will have net migration rates that are "next to zero." See Chapter 6 for a discussion of market ecologies

that examines the simultaneous effects of different levels of in- and out-migration. Another related problem has to do with our unit of analysis; that is, who we examine in the migration stream. While heads of households typically are the center of attention in most research designs, we have found that other household members, especially boarding relatives, have played a central role in the transformation of the rural economy. These migrants represented an important pool of labor that helped many farmers achieve a measure of success in the competitive surplus market economy. Although these migrants are virtually invisible using conventional migration data, the 1855 New York State Census once again allows us to examine their role in the process of change (see Chapter 7).

APPENDIX 1

1. Allan G. Bogue, *From Prairie to Corn Belt: Farming on the Illinois and Iowa Prairies in the Nineteenth Century.* (Chicago: University of Chicago Press, 1963), 26.

2. Ibid., 65, Table 9.

APPENDIX 2

1. Beef (consumed). All weight estimates were based on Morrison, *Feed and Feeding*, as well as contemporary estimates from *The Cultivator* and *The Northern Farmer*. The ratio of live animal to dressed meat (0.76) was derived from U.S. Department of Agriculture, "Conversion Factors"; Gallman, "Self-Sufficiency"; and Atack and Bateman, *To Their Own Soil* (p. 293, note 37). It was assumed that 7.6 pounds of dressed meat (net of hide, bones, etc.) was equivalent to 1 bushel of corn. This assumption was based on U.S. Department of Agriculture, "Conversion Factors"; and Atack and Bateman, *To Their Own Soil* (p. 293, note 37). Feed requirements came from U.S. Patent Office, *Reports* 1851–1856. Also see Atack and Bateman, *To Their Own Soil* (p. 210).

2. Swine (less than six months of age). Once again, weight estimates came from Morrison, *Feed and Feeding*, and contemporary evidence. See note 1 for dressed weight ratio and feed requirements. (The *New York State Census, 1865*, enumerated swine of all ages together.)

3. Swine (mature swine). See notes 1 and 2 for assumptions.

4. Neat cattle (less than six months of age and mature), working oxen, and horses. These animals were part of the working stock of the farm. See note 1 for feed estimates. (The *New York State Census, 1865*, distinguished between colts and horses.)

5. Working cows ("milk", "butter," and "cheese" cows). Here, only feed estimates were made. See note 1 above. For estimates of dairy production, see note 11 below.

6. Sheep. These animals typically were not consumed for their meat but were raised for their wool. See note 1 above for feed estimates. See note 13 below for conversions of wool to bushels of corn equivalents. (The *New York State Census, 1865*, distinguished between lambs and mature sheep. It also recorded the number of sheep "killed by dogs.")

7. Poultry (dollar value of poultry sold). Since poultry production was expressed in dollar value, its corn equivalence was estimated as an opportunity cost. The price of corn for this and all other opportunity cost conversions was based on S.E. Ronk, *Prices of Farm Products in New York State, 1841–1935;* and Atack and Bateman, *To Their Own Soil* (p. 234). Furthermore, Atack and Bateman assumed that an average 1855 chicken weighed four pounds (p. 231) and sold for 5.3 to 7.7 cents per pound. An average chicken, then, sold for about 25 cents. Again, estimates of feed requirements were based on Morrison, *Feed and Feeding*, and contemporary evidence from the agricultural press, especially *The Cultivator* and *The Northern Farmer*.

8. Spring wheat, winter wheat, barley, buckwheat, peas, beans, and oats all approxi-

mate corn in terms of caloric equivalents. This assumption came from Morrison, *Feed and Feeding*. Also see Atack and Bateman, *To Their Own Soil*, for estimates of seed requirements for all grain and root crops.

9. Rye, potatoes, and turnips were converted to corn equivalents as noted in note 8 above.

10. Hops was converted to corn equivalents on the basis of opportunity costs as noted in note 7 above.

11. Cheese, butter, and milk production were converted to corn equivalents derived from Morrison, *Feed and Feeding*.

12. Eggs were converted to corn equivalents on the basis of opportunity costs as noted in note 7 above.

13. All miscellaneous production was converted to corn equivalents on the basis of opportunity costs as noted in note 7 above. For conceptual clarity, those miscellaneous products reported as a quantity in the census were first converted into their dollar values and then into their corn equivalents.

14. Human consumption was expressed in corn equivalents. A diet of 5200 calories per day or 41.4 bushels of corn per year was assumed for an adult male (this includes estimates of waste and spoilage). This figure was derived from Atack and Bateman, *To Their Own Soil* (pp. 210, 224). Children were assumed to have 75 percent of the caloric needs of adult males. This represented an average for all children in the household, ranging from a figure of 15 percent of the adult male figure for children younger than four to 90 percent of the adult male figure for children eleven to fourteen years old. Adult females were assumed to have 90 percent of the adult male requirements. See U.S. Department of Commerce, Bureau of Labor, *Eighteenth Annual Report*, 1904, p. 102.

Bibliography

Abbott, John S.C. "George Washington." *Harper's New Monthly Magazine* 12 (February 1856): 289–315.

Abbott, Richard H. "The Agricultural Press Views the Yeoman 1819–1859." *Agricultural History* 42 (January 1968): 35–48.

Adams, Bret N. "Isolation, Function, and Beyond: American Kinship in the 1960s." *Journal of Marriage and the Family* 32 (November 1970): 575–97.

Adams, Henry. *The United States in 1800.* Ithaca: Great Seal Books, 1955.

Adams, John, and Alice Kasakoff. "Migration and the Family in Colonial New England: The View From Genealogies." *Journal of Family History* 9 (Spring 1984): 24–43.

Albion, Robert G. *The Rise of the New York Port, 1813–1860.* New York: C. Scribners and Sons, 1939.

Alcorn, Richard S. "Leadership and Stability in Mid-Nineteenth Century America: A Case Study of an Illinois Town." *Journal of American History* 61 (December 1974): 685–702.

American Agriculturist. 39 (August 1870): 30.

Anderson, Michael. *Family Structure in Nineteenth Century Lancashire.* Cambridge, U.K.: Cambridge University Press, 1971.

Appleby, Joyce. "Commercial Farming and the 'Agrarian Myth' in the Early Republic." *Journal of American History* 48 (1982): 833–35.

Atack, Jeremy. "Tenants and Yeomen in the Nineteenth Century." *Agricultural History* 62 (1988): 6–32.

Atack, Jeremy, and Fred Bateman. "The 'Egalitarian Ideal' and the Distribution of Wealth in the Northern Agricultural Community." *Review of Economics and Statistics* 63 (February 1981): 124–29.

———. "Egalitarianism, Inequality, and Age: The Rural North in 1860." *Journal of Economic History* 41 (March 1981): 85–93.

———. *To Their Own Soil: Agriculture in the Antebellum North.* Ames: Iowa State University Press, 1987.

Barber, John M., and Henry Howe. *Historical Collections of the State of New York.* Port Washington, N.Y.: S. Tuttle, 1841.

Barnett, H.G. *Innovations: The Basis of Cultural Change.* New York: McGraw-Hill, 1953.

Barron, Hal Seth. *Those Who Stayed Behind: Rural Society in Nineteenth Century New England.* New York: Cambridge University Press, 1984.

Barrows, Robert. "Hurryin' Hoosiers and the American 'Pattern': Geographic Mobility in Indianapolis and Urban North America." *Social Science History* 5 (1980): 197–222.

Bass, Bernard, and Ralph Alexander. "Climate, Economy, and the Differential Migration of White and Non-White Workers." *Journal of Applied Psychology* 56 (1972): 518–21.

Bateman, Fred. "The 'Marketable Surplus' in Northern Dairy Farming: New Evidence by Size of Farm in 1860." *Agricultural History* 52 (July 1978): 345–63.

Bateman, Fred, and Jeremy Atack. "The Profitability of Northern Agriculture in 1860." *Research in Economic History* 4 (1979): 87–125.

Bekaert, Geert. "Caloric Consumption in Industrializing Belgium." *Journal of Economic History* 51 (September 1991): 639.

Bennett, Merrill K., and Rosamond H. Pierce. "Changes in the American National Diet, 1879–1959." *Food Research Institute Studies* 2 (May 1961): 95–119.

Berkner, Lutz. "The Stem Family and the Developmental Cycle of the Peasant Household: An Eighteenth-Century Austrian Example." *American Historical Review* 77 (April 1972): 398–418.

Bernstein, Michael A., and Sean Wilentz. "Marketing, Commerce, and Capitalism in Rural Massachusetts." *Journal of Economic History* 44 (March 1984): 171–73.

Bidwell, Percy. "The Agricultural Revolution in New England." *American Historical Review* 26 (July 1921): 683–702.

Bidwell, Percy, and John Falconer. *History of Agriculture in the Northern States: 1620–1860.* Reprint. New York: Peter Smith, [1925], 1941.

Blake, John L. *The Family Textbook for the Country; or the Farmer at Home.* New York: C.M. Saxton, 1856.

Bliss, Porter. Diary, 1854. In the Bliss Family Papers. New York State Library Collection, Albany, N.Y.

Blumenthal, Albert B. *Small Town Stuff.* Chicago: University of Chicago Press, 1932.

Bogue, Allan G. *From Prairie to Corn Belt: Farming on the Illinois and Iowa Prairies in the Nineteenth Century.* Chicago: University of Chicago Press, 1963.

———. *Money at Interest: The Farm Mortgage on the Middle Border.* Ithaca: Cornell University Press, 1955.

Boorstin, Daniel. *The Genius of American Politics.* Chicago: University of Chicago Press, 1953.

Bouchard, Gerard. *SOREP Annual Reports.* (Inter-University Centre for Population Research, Gerard Bouchard, Director, Université du Québec à Chicoutimi.)

Bowers, William L. "Crawford Township, 1850–1870: A Population Study of a Pioneer Community." *Iowa Journal of History* 58 (January 1960): 7–30.

Brady, Dorothy. "Consumption and Style of Life." In *American Economic Growth: An Economist's History of the United States,* edited by Lance Davis, Richard Easterlin, and William Parker, 61–89. New York: Harper and Row, 1972.

———. "Relative Prices in the Nineteenth Century." *Journal of Economic History* 24 (June 1964): 145–203.

Brown, J., H. Swarzweller, and J. Mangalam. "Kentucky Mountain Migration and the Stem Family: An American Variation on a Theme by LePlay." *Rural Sociology* 28 (March 1963): 48–69.

Bruchey, Stuart. *The Roots of American Economic Growth, 1607–1861: An Essay in Social Causation.* New York: Harper and Row, 1965.

Brunger, Eric. "Dairying and Urban Development in New York State, 1850–1900." *Agricultural History* 29 (October 1955): 169–73.

Buck, Solon J. "Making Farms on the Frontier." *Agricultural History* 4 (July 1930): 92–120.

Burns, Rex. *Success in America: The Yeoman Dream and the Industrial Revolution.* Amherst: University of Massachusetts Press, 1976.

Calomiris, Charles W., and Larry Schweikart. "The Panic of 1857: Origins, Transmission, and Containment." *Journal of Economic History* 51 (December 1991): 807–34.

Carmer, Carl. *Genesee Fever.* New York: Farrar and Rinehart, Inc., 1941.

Carr, Lois Green, and Lorena S. Walsh. "Inventories and the Analysis of Wealth and Consumption Patterns in St. Mary's County, Maryland, 1658–1779." *Historical Methods* 13 (Spring 1980): 81–104.

Chevalier, Michel. *Society, Manners, and Politics in the United States,* edited by John W. Ward. Garden City: Doubleday, 1961.

Clark, Christopher. "The Household Economy, Market Exchange and the Rise of Capitalism in the Connecticut Valley, 1800–1860." *Journal of Social History* 13 (Fall 1979): 169–89.

———. *The Roots of Rural Capitalism, Western Massachusetts, 1780–1860.* Ithaca: Cornell University Press, 1990.

Clark, Colin, and M.R. Haswell. *The Economies of Subsistence Agriculture.* New York: St. Martin's Press, 1968.

Clark, Thomas D. *Pills, Petticoats, and Plows: The Southern Country Store, 1865–1900.* Norman: University of Oklahoma Press, 1944.

Coale, Ansley, and Melvin Zelnik. *New Estimates of Fertility and Population in the United States: A Study of Annual White Births from 1855 to 1960 and the Completeness of Enumeration in the Census from 1880 to 1960.* Princeton: Princeton University Press, 1963.

Cochran, Thomas. *Frontiers of Change: Early Industrialization in America.* New York: Oxford University Press, 1981.

Cogswell, Seddie, Jr. *Tenure Activity and Age as Factors in Iowa Agriculture, 1850–1880.* Ames: Iowa State University Press, 1975.

Coke, Edward Thomas. *A Subaltern's Furlough: Description of Scenes in Various Parts of the United States During the Summer and Autumn of 1832.* New York: J.J. Harper, 1833.

Colby, Merle Estes. *All Ye People*. New York: The Viking Press, 1931.

Cole, Arthur. *Business Enterprise in its Social Setting*. Cambridge, Mass.: Harvard University Press, 1959.

———. *Wholesale Commodity Prices, 1700–1861*. Cambridge, Mass: Harvard University Press, 1938.

Coleman, Gould P. "Innovation and Diffusion in Agriculture." *Agricultural History* 42 (July 1968): 173–87.

Coleman, Peter J. "Restless Grant County: America on the Move." *Wisconsin Magazine of History* 46 (Autumn 1962): 16–20.

Coleman, Peter T. *The Transformation of Rhode Island, 1790–1860*. Providence: Brown University Press, 1963.

Cook, Rice. *Diary of Rice Cook, 1854*. New York State Library Collections, Albany, N.Y.

Cooper, James Fennimore. *The Pioneers, or Sources of the Susquehanna*. New York: Wiley, 1823.

Courchene, T.J. "Interprovincial Migration and Economic Adjustment." *Canadian Journal of Economics* 3 (November 1970): 550–75.

Craig, Lee. "The Value of Household Labor in Antebellum Northern Agriculture." *Journal of Economic History* 51 (March 1991): 67–81.

———. *To Sow One Acre More*. Baltimore: Johns Hopkins University Press, 1993.

Cross, Whitney. *The Burned-Over District*. Ithaca: Cornell University Press, 1950.

The Cultivator. Issues from 1848 to 1857.

Cummings, Richard. *The American and His Food: A History of Food Habits in the United States*. Chicago: University of Chicago Press, 1940.

Curti, Merle. *The Making of an American Community: A Case Study of Democracy in a Frontier County*. Stanford: Stanford University Press, 1959.

———. *The Social Ideas of American Educators*. New York: C. Scribner's Sons, 1935.

Danbom, David. *The Resisted Revolution: Urban America and the Industrialization of Agriculture*. Ames: Iowa State University Press, 1979.

Danhof, Clarence. "The Farm Enterprise: The Northern United States, 1820–1860s." *Research in Economic History* 4 (1979): 127–91.

———. "The Tools and Implements of Agriculture." *Agricultural History* 46 (January 1972): 81–90.

Darroch, Gordon. "Migrants in the Nineteenth Century: Fugitives or Families in Motion." *Journal of Family History* 6 (Fall 1981): 257–77.

Davenport, David Paul. "Population Persistence and Migration in Rural New York, 1855–1860." Ph.D. diss., University of Illinois, 1983.

Davis, Rodney O. "Prairie Emporium: Clarence, Iowa, 1860–1880: A Study of Population Trends." *Mid-America* 51 (April 1969): 130–39.

Demaree, Albert L. *The American Agricultural Press, 1819–1860*. Morningside Heights, N.Y.: Columbia University Press, 1941.

———. "The Farm Journals, Their Editors, and Their Public, 1830–1860." *Agricultural History* 15 (October 1941): 182–88.

Demos, John. "Families in Colonial Bristol, Rhode Island: An Exercise in Historical Demography." *William and Mary Quarterly,* 3rd series 25 (January 1968): 40–57.

Dublin, Thomas. "Women and Outwork in a Nineteenth Century New England Town." In *The Countryside in the Age of Capitalist Transformation*, edited by Steven Hahn and Jonathan Prude, 51-69. Chapel Hill: University of North Carolina Press, 1985.

Duffy, John, and H. Nicholas Mullen, III. *An Anxious Democracy: Aspects of the 1830s*. Westport, Conn.: Greenwood Press, 1982.

Easterlin, Richard A., George Alter, and Gretchen Condran. "Farm Families in Old and New Areas: The Northern United States in 1860." In *Family and Population in Nineteenth Century America*, edited by Tamara Hareven and Maris A. Vinovskis, 22–84. Princeton: Princeton University Press, 1978.

Ellis, David Maldwyn. *Landlords and Farmers in the Hudson-Mohawk Region, 1790–1850*. Ithaca: Cornell University Press, 1946.

Engels, Frederick. *The Origins of the Family, Private Property, and the State*. New York: International Publishing Co., 1972.

"Farmer A or the Rolling Stone by A Traveler," *The Genesee Farmer,* 23 July 1836, 236.

Farrell, Richard. "Advice to Farmers: The Content of Agricultural Newspapers, 1860–1910." *Agricultural History* 51 (January 1977): 209–17.

Fish, Carl Russell. *The Rise of the Common Man*. New York: The MacMillan Co., 1927.

Fisher, Marvin. *Workshops in the Wilderness: The European Response to American Industrialization, 1830–1860*. New York: Oxford University Press, 1967.

Fishlow, Albert. *American Railroads and the Transformation of the Antebellum Economy*. Cambridge, Mass.: Harvard University Press, 1965.

―――. "Antebellum Interregional Trade Reconsidered." In *New Views on American Economic Development*, edited by Ralph Andreano. Cambridge, Mass.: Harvard University Press, 1965.

Fogel, Robert. "Biomedical Approaches to the Estimation and Interpretation of Secular Trends in Equity, Morbidity, Mortality and Labor Productivity in Europe, 1750–1980." University of Chicago, mimeo, 1987. Cited in Geert Bekaert, "Caloric Consumption in Industrializing Belgium." *Journal of Economic History* 51 (September 1991): 639, Table 3.

Freedman, Ronald. "Health Differentials for Rural-Urban Migration." *American Sociological Review* 12 (1974): 536–41.

Furstenburg, Frank. "Industrialization and the American Family: A Look Backward." *American Sociological Review* 31 (June 1966) 326–37.

Furstenburg, Frank, Douglas Strong, and Albert G. Crawford. "What Happened When the Census Was Redone: An Analysis of the Recount of 1870 in Philadelphia." *Sociology and Social Research* 61 (1979): 475–505.

Gagan, David P., and Herbert Mays. "Historical Demography and Canadian Social History: Family and Land in Peel County, Ontario." *Canadian Historical Review* 14 (March 1973): 27–47.

Galenson, David. "Economic Determinants of the Age at Leaving Home: Evidence From the Lives of Nineteenth Century New England Manufacturers." *Social Science History* 11 (Winter 1987): 355–78.

―――. "Economic and Geographic Mobility on the Farming Frontier." *Journal of Economic History* (September 1989): 635–55.

Gallman, Robert E. "Commodity Output, 1839–1899." In *Trends in the American Economy in the Nineteenth Century*. Conference on Income and Wealth. Princeton: Princeton University Press, 1960.

———. "Self Sufficiency in the Cotton Economy of the Antebellum South." *Agricultural History* 44 (January 1970): 5–24.

———. *Recent Developments in the Study of Business and Economic History. Essays in Memory of Herman E. Kross*. Greenwich, Conn.: JAI Press, 1977.

Garland, Hamlin. *Main-Travelled Roads*. New York: Harper and Bros., 1899.

Gates, Paul W. *The Farmer's Age: Agriculture 1815–1860*. New York: Holt, Rinehart, and Winston, 1960.

———. "The Homestead Law in Iowa." *Agricultural History* 38 (April 1964): 67–78.

———. "Agricultural Change in New York State." *New York History* 50 (April 1969): 115–41.

———. "Problems of Agricultural History." *Agricultural History* 46 (January 1972): 37.

The Genesee Farmer. Issues from 1838 to 1844.

Glasco, Laurence. "Migration and Adjustment in the Nineteenth Century City: Occupation, Property, and Household Structure of Native Born Whites, Buffalo, New York, 1855." In *Family and Population in Nineteenth Century America*, edited by Tamara Hareven and Maris Vinovskis. Princeton: Princeton University Press, 1978.

Goldstein, Sidney. *Patterns of Mobility, 1910–1950: The Norristown Survey*. Philadelphia: University of Pennsylvania Press, 1958.

Goodrich, Carter. *Government Promotion of American Canals and Railroad*. New York: Columbia University Press, 1960.

Gráda, Cormac Ó. *Ireland: A New Economic History, 1780–1939*. Oxford: Oxford University Press, 1994. Cited in Geert Bekaert, "Caloric Consumption in Industrializing Belgium." *Journal of Economic History* 51 (September 1991): 639, Table 3.

Green, Lois, and Lorena Walsh. "Toward a History of the Standard of Living in British North America." *William and Mary Quarterly* 45 (January 1988): 116–70.

Greenwood, M.J., and I. Gormerly. "A Comparison of the Determinants of White and Non-White Migration." *Demography* 8 (February 1971): 141–55.

Gregson, Mary Eschelbach. "Strategies for Commercialization: Missouri Agriculture, 1860–1880." Ph.D. diss., University of Illinois at Urbana-Champaign, 1993.

Griffen, Clyde. "Workers Divided: The Effect of Craft and Ethnic Differences in Poughkeepsie, New York: 1850–1880." In *Nineteenth Century Cities: Essays in New Urban History*, edited by Stephan Thernstrom and Richard Sennett. New Haven: Yale University Press, 1969.

Gue, Benjamin. *The Diary of Benjamin Gue, 1851–1865*. New York State Library Collections, Albany, N.Y.

Gutman, Herbert. *The Black Family in Slavery and Freedom: 1750–1925*. New York: Pantheon Books, 1976.

Gutmann, Myron. "The Future of Record Linkage in History." *Journal of Family*

History 2 (1977): 151–57.

Hackley, Delos. *Diary of Delos Hackley,* 1849–1875. Private collection.

Hahn, Steven, and Jonathan Prude, eds. *The Countryside in the Age of Capitalist Transformation.* Chapel Hill: University of North Carolina, 1985.

Handlin, Oscar. *The Uprooted.* Boston: Little, Brown, 1951.

Hareven, Tamara K. "The Family as Process: The Historical Study of the Family Cycle." *Journal of Social History* 7 (Spring 1974): 322–29.

———. "The History of the Family and the Complexity of Social Change." *American Historical Review* 96 (February 1991): 95–124.

Hareven, Tamara, and Randolph Langenbach. *Amoskeag: Life and Work in an American Factory City.* New York: Pantheon Books, 1980.

Hartz, Louis. *The Liberal Tradition in America.* New York: Harcourt Brace, 1955.

Hayter, Earl. *The Troubled Farmer, 1850–1900: Rural Adjustment to Industrialism.* DeKalb: Northern Illinois University Press, 1968.

Hedrick, Ulysses Prentiss. *A History of Agriculture in the State of New York.* Albany: New York State Agricultural Society, 1933.

———. "What Farmers Read in Western New York, 1800–1850." *New York History* 17 (July 1936): 281–89.

Henretta, James. "Families and Farm: Mentalite in Pre-Industrial America." *William and Mary Quarterly,* 3rd series, 35 (January 1978): 3–32.

Henry, W.A. *Feeds and Feeding: A Handbook for the Student and Stockman.* 5th ed. Madison, Wis: by the author, 1903.

Hofstadter, Richard. *The Age of Reform: From Bryan to FDR.* New York: Vintage Books, 1955.

———. "The Myth of the Happy Yeoman." *American Heritage* 7 (April 1956): 43–53.

———. *The Progressive Historians.* New York: Vintage Books, 1968.

Hoke, Donald R. *Ingenious Yankees: The Rise of the American System of Manufactures in the Private Sector.* New York: Columbia University Press, 1990.

Holbrook, William. *Diary of William Holbrook, 1854.* New York State Library Collections, Albany, N.Y.

Hopkins, Richard J. "Occupational and Geographic Mobility in Atlanta, 1860–1896." *Journal of Southern History* 34 (May 1968): 200–13.

Hopkins, Samuel Adams. *Canal Town.* New York: Random House, 1944.

Houndshell, David A. *From American System to Mass Production, 1800–1837: The Development of Manufacturing Technology in the United States.* Baltimore: Johns Hopkins University Press, 1984.

House Document No. 136, In *Andrews Report on Colonial and Lake Trade, 1852.* Washington, D.C.: U.S. GPO, 1853.

Howison, John. *Sketches of Upper Canada: Domestic, Local, and Characteristics and Some Recollections of the United States of America.* Edinburgh: S.R. Publishers, 1822.

Huston, James L. *The Panic of 1857 and the Coming of the Civil War.* Baton Rouge: Louisiana State University Press, 1987.

Inkles, Alex, and David Smith. *Becoming Modern.* Cambridge, U.K.: Cambridge University Press, 1974.

Jaffee, David. "Peddlers of Progress and the Transformation of the Rural North."

Journal of American History 78 (September 1991): 511–35.

Jefferson, Thomas. *Notes on Virginia*. Reprinted in Richard Hofstadter, *Great Issues in American History*. Vol. 2. New York: Vintage, 1958, 169–70.

Katz, Michael. *The People of Hamilton, Canada West: Family and Class in a Mid-Nineteenth Century City*. Cambridge, U.K.: Cambridge University Press, 1975.

Katz, Michael, and J. Tiller. "Record Linkage for Everyman: A Semi-Automated Process." *Historical Methods* 5 (1975): 144–50.

Katz, Michael, Michael Doucet, and Mark Stern. "Migration and the Social Order in Erie County, New York, 1855." *Journal of Interdisciplinary History* 8 (1978): 669–702.

———. *The Social Organization of Early Industrial Capitalism*. Cambridge, Mass.: Harvard University Press, 1982.

Kertzer, David, and Dennis Hogan. "Surviving Kin and Coresidence in a Nineteenth Century Italian Town." Paper presented at Social Science History Association Meetings, Fall 1990.

Kessner, Thomas. *The Golden Door: Italian and Jewish Immigrant Mobility in New York City, 1880–1915*. New York: Oxford University Press, 1977.

Kirk, Gordon W., and Carol Kirk. "Migration, Mobility, and Transformation of Occupational Structure in an Immigrant Community: Holland, Michigan, 1850–1880." *Journal of Social History* 7 (Winter 1974): 142–64.

Knights, Peter. *The Plain People of Boston, 1830–1860: A Study in City Growth*. New York: Oxford University Press, 1971.

———. *Yankee Destinies*. Chapel Hill: University of North Carolina Press, 1991.

Knights, Peter, and Richard S. Alcorn. "Most Uncommon Bostonians: A Critique of Stephan Thernstrom's *The Other Bostonians: Poverty and Progress in the American Metropolis: 1850–1970*." *Historical Methods* 8 (Fall 1975): 98–114.

Komlos, John. *Nutrition and Economic Development in the Eighteenth Century, Hapsburg Monarchy: An Anthropometric History*. Princeton: Princeton University Press, 1990.

Kulik, Gary. "Dams, Fish, and Farmers: Defense of Public Rights in Eighteenth-Century Rhode Island." In *The Countryside in the Age of Capitalist Transformation: Essays in the Social History of Rural America*, edited by Steven Hahn and Jonathan Prude. Chapel Hill: University of North Carolina Press, 1985.

Kulikoff, Allan. *The Agrarian Origins of American Capitalism*. Charlottesville: University Press of Virginia, 1992.

Kuznets, Simon Smith, and Dorothy Swain Thomas, eds. *Population Redistribution and Economic Growth, 1870–1950*. Philadelphia: American Philosophical Society, 1957.

Lansing, John B., and Eva Mueller. *The Geographic Mobility of Labor*. Ann Arbor: Survey Research Center, University of Michigan, 1967.

Lantz, Herman R., and Ernest K. Alix. "Occupational Mobility in a Nineteenth-Century Mississippi Valley River Community." *Social Science Quarterly* 51 (September 1970): 404–08.

Laslett, Peter. "Characteristics of the Western Family Over Time." In *Family Life and Illicit Love in Earlier Generations: Essays in Historical Sociology,* edited by Peter Laslett. Cambridge: Cambridge University Press, 1977.

Laslett, Peter, and Richard Wall, eds. *Household and Family in Past Time.* New York: Cambridge University Press, 1972.

Lebergott, Stanley. "Migration Within the U.S., 1800–1960: Some New Estimates." *Journal of Economic History* 30 (1970): 839–46.

Lee, Everett. "The Turner Thesis Reexamined." *American Quarterly* 13 (Spring 1961): 77–83.

Lemmer, George F. "Early Agricultural Editors and Their Philosophies. *Agricultural History* 31 (October 1957): 3–22.

Lemon, James T. *The Best Poor Man's Country: A Geographical Study of Early Southeastern Pennsylvania.* Baltimore: Johns Hopkins University Press, 1972.

———. "Early Americans and Their Social Environment." *Journal of Historical Geography* 6 (April 1980): 115–31.

———. "Comment on James T. Henretta's Families in Pre-Industrial America." *William and Mary Quarterly,* 3rd series, 37 (October 1980): 688–96.

———. "Household Consumption in Eighteenth Century America and its Relationship to Production and Trade: The Situation Among Farmers in Southeastern Pennsylvania." *Agricultural History* 41 (January 1967): 59–70.

LePlay, Frederick. *On Family, Work, and Social Change.* Chicago: University of Chicago Press, 1982.

Levenstein, Harvey. *Revolution at the Table: The Transformation of the American Diet.* New York: Oxford University Press, 1988.

Lindstrom, Diane L. "Demand Markets and Eastern Economic Development, Philadelphia 1815–1840." *Journal of Economic History* 35 (March 1975): 271–73.

———. "Southern Dependence upon Interregional Grain Supplies: A Review of Trade Flows, 1840–1860." *Agricultural History* 44 (January 1970): 101–13.

Locke, Harvey J. "Mobility and Family Disorganization." *American Sociological Review* 5 (August 1940): 489–94.

Loehr, Rodney. "Moving Back from the Atlantic Seaboard." *Agricultural History* 17 (April 1943): 90–96.

———. "Self-Sufficiency on the Farm." *Agricultural History* 26 (April 1952): 37–41.

MacDonald, J., and L. MacDonald. "Chain Migration, Ethnic Neighborhood Formation, and Social Networks." *Milbank Memorial Fund Quarterly* 42 (January 1964): 82–93.

Main, Jackson Turner. *The Social Structure of Revolutionary America.* Princeton: Princeton University Press, 1965.

Malin, James C. "The Turnover of Farm Population in Kansas." *Kansas Historical Quarterly* 4 (1935): 339–72. Reprinted in Robert Swierenga, ed., *History and Ecology: Studies of Grassland.* Lincoln: University of Nebraska Press, 1984.

Malzberg, Benjamin. "Migration and Mental Disease Among Negroes in New York State." *American Journal of Physical Anthropology* 2 (January 1936): 107–13.

———. "Rates of Mental Disease Among Certain Population in New York State." *Journal of the American Statistical Association* 31 (September 1936): 547.

Mann, Ralph. "The Decade After the Gold Rush: Social Structure in Grass Valley and Nevada City, California, 1850–1860." *Pacific Historical Review* 41 (November 1972): 484–504.

Marti, Donald. "Agricultural Journalism and the Diffusion of Knowledge: The First Half Century in America." *Agricultural History* 54 (January 1980): 28–37.

Martin, Edgar W. *The Standard of Living in 1860: American Consumption Levels on the Eve of the Civil War*. Chicago: University of Chicago Press, 1942.

Matthews, Lois K. *The Expansion of New England: The Spread of New England Settlement and Institutions to the Mississippi River*. New York: Russell and Russell, 1962.

McGrane, Reginald Charles. *The Panic of 1837: Some Financial Problems of the Jacksonian Era*. Chicago: University of Chicago Press, 1965.

McInnis, Marvin. "Marketable Surpluses in Ontario Farming." *Social Science History* 8 (Fall 1984): 395–424.

McNall, Neil Adams. *An Agricultural History of the Genesee Valley, 1790–1860*. Philadelphia: University of Pennsylvania Press, 1952.

———. "John Greig: Land Agent and Speculator." *Business History Review* 33 (Winter 1959): 524–34.

Mellor, John. "Use and Productivity of Farm Family Labor in the Early Stages of Agricultural Development." *Journal of Farm Economics* 45 (August 1963): 517–34.

Merrill, Michael. "Cash is Good to Eat: Self-Sufficiency and Exchange in the Rural Economy of the United States." *Radical History Review* 3 (1977): 43–71.

Meyers, Marvin. *The Jacksonian Persuasion: Politics and Beliefs*. Palo Alto, Calif.: Stanford University Press, 1957.

Miller, Roberta Balstead. *City and Hinterland: A Case Study of Urban Growth and Regional Development*. Westport, Conn.: Greenwood Press, 1979.

Monkkonen, Eric, ed. "Introduction." *Walking to Work: Tramps in America, 1790–1935*. Lincoln: University of Nebraska Press, 1984.

Morrison, F.B. *Feed and Feeding*. 20th ed. Ithaca: Morrison Publishing Co., 1936.

Morrison, Peter. "Chronic Movers and the Future Redistribution of the Population." *Demography* 8 (May 1971): 171–84.

Morrison, Peter, and Judith Wheeler. "The Image of 'Elsewhere' in the American Tradition of Migration." In *Human Migration: Patterns and Policies*, edited by William McNeill and Ruthe Adams. Bloomington: Indiana University Press, 1978.

Mowrer, Ernest R. *Family Disorganization: An Introduction to Sociological Analysis*. Chicago: University of Chicago Press, 1927.

———. *The Family: Its Organization and Disorganization*. Chicago: University of Chicago Press, 1932.

Mowrer, Ernest R., and Pauline Young. "The Reorganization of the Jewish Family Life in America: A Natural History of Social Forces Governing the Assimilation of the Jewish Immigrant," *Social Forces* (December 1928): 213–43.

Mutch, Robert. "The Cutting Edge: Colonial America and the Debate About the Transition to Capitalism." *Theory and Society* 9 (November 1980): 847–63.

———. "Yeoman and Merchant in Pre-Industrial America." *Societas* 7 (Autumn 1977): 279–302.

New York State. *Census of the State of New York, 1855.* Prepared by Franklin B. Hough. Albany, N.Y.: Charles Van Benthurysen, 1857.

New York State. Manuscript Census of the State of New York, 1855. Albany, N.Y.: 1855 Population and Agricultural Schedules.

———. Albany County, N.Y.

———. Broome County, N.Y.

———. Cattaraugus County, N.Y.

———. Chemung County, N.Y.

———. Chenango County, N.Y.

———. Delaware County, N.Y.

———. Erie County, N.Y.

———. Essex County, N.Y.

———. Fulton County, N.Y.

———. Greene County, N.Y.

———. Herkimer County, N.Y.

———. Jefferson County, N.Y.

———. Livingston County, N.Y.

———. Lewis County, N.Y.

———. Madison County, N.Y.

———. Monroe County, N.Y.

———. Onondaga County, N.Y.

———. Ontario County, N.Y.

———. Orange County, N.Y.

———. Orleans County, N.Y.

———. Oswego County, N.Y.

———. Rensselaer County, N.Y.

———. Saratoga County, N.Y.

———. Sullivan County, N.Y.

———. Ulster County, N.Y.

———. Washington County, N.Y.

New York State. Manuscript Census of the State of New York, 1865. Albany, N.Y.: 1865 Population and Agricultural Schedules.

———. Broome County, N.Y.

———. Cattaraugus County, N.Y.

———. Greene County, N.Y.

———. Lewis County, N.Y.

———. Monroe County, N.Y.

———. Onondaga County, N.Y.

———. Rensselaer County, N.Y.

———. Washington County, N.Y.

———. Yates County, N.Y.

Nobles, Gregory. "Capitalism in the Countryside: The Transformation of Rural Society in the United States." *Radical History Review* 41 (1988): 163–76.

North, Douglass. *The Economic Growth of the United States, 1790–1860.* Englewood Cliffs, N.J.: Prentice Hall, 1961.

The Northern Farmer. Issues from 1855 to 1857.

Oberly, James. *Ten Million Acres.* Kent, Ohio: Kent State University Press, 1989.

Ogburn, William F. *Technology and the Changing Family.* Boston: Houghton Mifflin, 1955.

Osterud, Nancy Grey. *Bonds of Community.* Ithaca: Cornell University Press, 1991.

Park, Robert E., Ernest Burgess, and Roderick McKenzie. *The City.* Chicago: University of Chicago Press, 1925.

Parker, William N. "Sources of Agricultural Productivity in the Nineteenth-Century." *Journal of Farm Economics* 49 (December 1967): 1455–68.

Parker, William, and Judith L.V. Klein. "Productivity Growth in Grain Production in the U.S., 1840–1860 and 1900–1910." In *Output Employment and Productivity in the United States After 1800.* Edited by Dorothy S. Brady. Cambridge, Mass.: National Bureau of Economic Research, 1966.

Parkerson, Donald H. "Comments on Underenumeration of the U.S. Census, 1850–1880." *Social Science History* 15 (1991): 509–19.

———. "How Mobile Were Nineteenth Century Americans?" *Historical Methods* 15 (Summer 1982): 99–109.

———. "The People of New York State in Mid Nineteenth Century: Community, Household and Migration." Ph.D. Diss., University of Illinois, 1983.

———, ed. Series of articles on "Underenumeration of the U.S. Census, 1850–1880." In *Social Science History* 15 (1991): 509–602.

Parkerson, Donald H., and Jo Ann Parkerson. "Estimating the Population Dynamics of New York State at Mid-Nineteenth Century: A Group-Event Approach." Paper presented at the Social Science History Association Meetings, Chicago, 1989.

Parrington, Vernon Louis. *Main Currents in American Thought,* Vols. I and II. New York: Harcourt Brace, 1954.

Parsons, Talcott. *Family Socialization and Interaction Process.* Glencoe, Ill.: Free Press, 1955.

———. "The Kinship System of the Contemporary United States." *American Anthropologist* 45 (1943): 22–38.

Paul, David. "The Mechanization of Reaping in the Antebellum Midwest." In *Industrialization in Two Systems,* edited by Henry Rosovsky. New York: Wiley, 1966.

Perkins, Elizabeth. "The Consumer Frontier: Household Consumption in Early Kentucky." *Journal of American History* 78 (September 1991): 487.

Pierson, George. *The Moving American.* New York: Knopf, 1973.

Porter, Glenn, and Harold Livesay. *Merchants and Manufacturers: Studies in the Changing Structure of Nineteenth-Century Marketing.* Baltimore: Johns Hopkins University Press, 1971.

Prest, W.R. "Stability and Change in Old and New England: Clayworth and Dedham." *Journal of Interdisciplinary History* 6 (Winter 1976): 359–74.

Prude, Jonathan. *The Coming of Industrial Order: Town and Factory Life in Rural Massachusetts 1810–1860.* New York: Cambridge University Press, 1983.

Pruitt, Bettye Hobbs. "Self-Sufficiency and the Agricultural Economy of Massachusetts." *William and Mary Quarterly* 41 (July 1984): 333–64.

Ralston, Leonard F. "Migration and Settlement: Courtland County 1855." Paper presented to the New York State Studies Group Meeting, Brockport, June 1978.

Ravenstein, E.G. "The Laws of Migration: First Paper." *Journal of the Royal Statistical Society* 48 (1885).

———. "The Laws of Migration: Second Paper." *Journal of the Royal Statistical Society* 52 (1889).

Raymond, Richard. "Determinants of Non-White Migration During the 1950s: Their Regional Significance and Long Term Implications." *American Journal of Economic Sociology* 31 (January 1972): 9–20.

Rikoon, J. Stanford. *Threshing in the Midwest, 1820–1940*. Bloomington: Indiana University Press, 1988.

Robbins, William G. "Opportunity and Persistence in the Pacific Northwest: A Quantitative Study of Early Roseburg, Oregon." *Pacific Historical Review* 39 (August 1970): 279–96.

Roberts, Isaac Phillips. *Autobiography of a Farm Boy*. Ithaca: Cornell University Press, 1946.

Rogin, Leo. *The Introduction of Farm Machinery and its Relation to the Productivity of Labor in the Agriculture of the United States during the Nineteenth Century*. Berkeley: University of California Press, 1931.

Ronk, S.E. *Prices of Farm Products in New York State, 1841 to 1935*. Ithaca: Cornell University Agricultural Station No. 643, 1936.

Rothenberg, Winifred. "The Market and Massachusetts, 1750–1855." *Journal of Economic History* 41 (March 1981): 283–314.

———. "The Emergence of a Capital Market in Rural Massachusetts, 1730–1838." *Journal of Economic History* 45 (December 1985): 781–808.

———. *From Market-Place to a Market Economy*. Chicago: University of Chicago Press, 1992.

Rothstein, Morten. "Antebellum Wheat and Cotton Exports." *Agricultural History* 40 (April 1966): 91–100.

Ruggles, Steven. "Availability of Kin and the Demography of Historical Family Structure." *Historical Methods* 19 (Summer 1986): 93–102.

———. "The Transformation of American Family Structure." *American Historical Review* 99 (1994): 103–28.

Ryan, Mary. *Cradle of the Middle Class: The Family in Oneida County, New York, 1790–1865*. New York: Cambridge University Press, 1981.

Seward, R. "Household versus Family Membership in the United States: Historical Trends." Paper presented at the American Sociological Association, Chicago, 1977.

Shammas, Carole. "How Self-Sufficient was Early America?" *Journal of Interdisciplinary History* 13 (Autumn 1982): 247–72.

———. "The Eighteenth Century English Diet and Economic Change." *Explorations in Economic History* 21 (July 1984): 254–69.

———. *The Pre-Industrial Consumer in England and America*. Oxford, U.K.: Oxford University Press, 1990.

Shaw, Ronald. *Erie Water West: A History of the Erie Canal.* Lexington: University of Kentucky Press, 1966.

Sherman, Rexford. "Daniel Webster Gentleman Farmer." *Agricultural History* 53 (April 1979): 475–87.

Shorter, Edward. *The Making of the Modern Family.* New York: Basic Books, 1975.

Simler, Lucy. "The Landless Worker: An Index of Economic and Social Change in Chester County, Pennsylvania, 1750–1820." *Pennsylvania Magazine of History and Biography* 114 (April 1990): 163–99.

Simmel, Georg. *The Sociology of Georg Simmel.* Edited by Kurt Wolff. New York: The Free Press, 1950.

Smith, Daniel Scott. "The Curious History of Theorizing About the History of the Western Nuclear Family." *Social Science History* 17 (1993): 325–53.

Smith, David C. "Middle Range Farming in the Civil War Era: Life on a Farm in Seneca County, 1862–1866." *New York History* 48 (October 1967): 352–69.

Smith, Kathleen. "Moore's Rural New Yorker: A Farm Program for the 1850's." *Agricultural History* 45 (January 1971): 39–46.

Smith, Walter B., and Arthur Cole. *Fluctuations in American Business, 1790–1860.* Cambridge, Mass.: Harvard University Press, 1935.

Sommers, P.M., and D.B. Suits, "Analysis of Net Interstate Migration." *Southern Economic Journal* 40 (October 1973): 193–201.

Stephenson, Charles. "Tracing Those Who Left: Mobility Studies and the Sound Indexes to the U.S. Census." *Journal of Urban History* 1 (1977): 73–84.

Stuart, James. *Three Years in North America.* Edinburgh: R. Cadell, 1833.

Swierenga, Robert. "Theoretical Perspectives on the New Rural History: From Environmentalism to Modernization." *Agricultural History* 56 (January 1982): 495–502.

Tarver, James D., and William R. Gurley. "The Relationship of Selected Variables with County Net Migration Rates in the United States, 1950–1960." *Rural Sociology* 30 (March 1965): 3–13.

Taylor, Alan. *Liberty Men and Great Proprietors.* Chapel Hill: University of North Carolina Press, 1990.

Temin, Peter. *Causal Factors in American Economic Growth in the 19th Century.* London: MacMillan, 1975.

———. *The Jacksonian Economy.* New York: Norton, 1969.

Thernstrom, Stephan. *The Other Bostonians: Poverty and Progress in the American Metropolis, 1880–1970.* Cambridge, Mass.: Harvard University Press, 1973.

———. *Poverty and Progress: Social Mobility in a Nineteenth Century City.* Cambridge, Mass.: Harvard University Press, 1964.

Thernstrom, Stephan, and Peter Knights. "Men in Motion: Some Speculations about Urban Population Mobility in the Nineteenth Century." In *Anonymous Americans: Explorations in Nineteenth-Century Social History,* edited by Tamara K. Hareven. Englewood Cliffs, N.J.: Prentice Hall, 1971.

Thomas, W.I., and Florien Znanecki. *The Polish Peasant in Europe and America.* 2

vols. Boston: R.G. Badger, 1918.

Thompson, E.P. "Time, Work-Discipline, and Industrial Capitalism." *Past and Present* 38 (December 1967): 56–97.

Thompson, F.M.L. "The Second Agricultural Revolution, 1815–1880." *Economic History Review* 21 (April 1968): 62–77.

Thompson, William. *A Tradesman's Travels in the United States and Canada in the Years 1840, 41, and 42*. Edinburgh: Oliver and Boyd, 1842.

Tobey, Ronald, Charles Wetherell, and Jay Brigham. "Moving Out and Settling In: Residential Mobility, Homeowning, and the Public Enframing of Citizenship, 1921–1950." *American Historical Review* 95 (December 1990): 1395–1422.

de Tocqueville, Alexis. *Democracy in America*. New York: Vintage Books, 1945.

Tönnies, Ferdinand. *Community and Society*. Edited and translated by Charles Loomes. East Lansing: Michigan State University Press, 1957.

Tryon, Rolla M. *Household Manufactures in the United States, 1646–1860: A Study in Industrial History*. Chicago: University of Chicago Press, 1917.

Turner, Frederick Jackson. *Rise of the New West*. New York: Harper and Bros., 1906.

———. "The Significance of the Frontier in American History." In *The Turner Thesis Concerning the Role of the Frontier in American History*, edited by George Rogers Taylor. Boston: Heath, 1941.

U.S. Bureau of the Census. *Historical Statistics: Colonial Times to 1957*. Washington, D.C.: U.S. GPO, 1960.

U.S. Bureau of the Census Statistical Research Division. *The Statistical History of the United States from Colonial Times to the Present*. New York: Basic Books, 1976.

U.S. Department of Agriculture. "Conversion Factors and Weights and Measures for Agricultural Commodities and Their Products." *Statistical Bulletin* 362. Washington D.C.: U.S. GPO, 1965.

U.S. Department of Commerce, Bureau of Labor. *Eighteenth Annual Report*. Washington D.C.: U.S. GPO, 1904.

Van Orden, William. *Account Book of William Van Orden, April and May 1860*. New York State Library Collections, Albany, N.Y.

Wallace, Henry A. *Agricultural Prices*. Des Moines: Wallace Publishing Co., 1920.

Ware, Norman. *The Industrial Worker, 1840–1860: The Reaction of American Industrial Society to the Advance of the Industrial Revolution*. Gloucester, Mass.: Peter Smith, 1959.

Westcott, Edward. *David Harum: A Story of American Life*. New York: D. Appleton, 1899.

Wilder, Laura Ingalls. *Farmer Boy*. New York: Harper, 1933.

Williamson, Jeffrey G., and Peter H. Lindert. *American Inequality: A Macroeconomic History*. New York: Academic Press, 1980.

Winchester, Ian. "The Linkage of Historical Records by Man and Computer: Techniques and Problems." *Journal of Interdisciplinary History* (Autumn 1970): 107–25.

Wines, Richard. "The Nineteenth Century Agricultural Transition in an Eastern

Long Island Community." *Agricultural History* 55 (January 1981): 50–63.

Wirth, Louis. "Urbanism as a Way of Life." *American Journal of Sociology* 44 (1938): 1–24.

Yang, Donghyu. "Notes on the Wealth Distribution of Farm Households in the United States 1860: A New Look at Two Manuscript Samples." *Explorations in Economic History* 21 (January 1984): 88–102.

Yans-McLaughlin, Virginia. *Family and Community: Italian Immigrants in Buffalo, 1880–1930.* Ithaca: Cornell University Press, 1977.

Zelinsky, Wilbur. "The Hypothesis of the Mobility Transition." *Geographical Review* 61 (April 1971): 219–49.

Index